AF588167

The Book of Na

Na Mira

Wendy's Subway

Contents

How to

AKE A TESSERAC

2012/12/06

i remember the book in my purse and ask my parents if they want me to read aloud. he demands to see it first and then reads from Clarice Lispector for an hour. *So hear me with your whole body... When you come to read me you will ask why I don't keep to painting and my exhibitions since I write so rough and disorderly. It's because now I feel the need for words and what I'm writing is new to me because until now my true word has never been touched. The word is my fourth dimension.* he lays *Água Viva* down on the hospital bed and says, *This is absolute bullshit.* Nayop says it sounds like i could be writing this kind of book.

BROOKE INTRACHAT

CHIRON

SAI ANANTAM ASHRAM

TUTANKHAMUN

GLITCH

TIGER

CHINOISERIE DRAGON CHAIR

AND LET ME TELL YOU IT WAS WONDERFUL

a smeared candle cut in half like a teenager

bruised eyes blush seeing through flowers

metal tail ascends from shackle

I HAVE BEEN TO HELL AND BACK

the shaman doubled in black and white, above

she stands on a bridge painting their holes

HANUMAN

WATERFALL

HOLOGRAM

HOLE IN MY FOOT

MU

ABD AL-RAHMAN AL-SUFI CONSTELLATIONS

CROSS

scissors, smoke, incense, ink

green brushstrokes from the throat

a painting of a photograph of a flame cut at its point

Kusama's *self-obliteration* arching across sky

the shaman doubled in black and white, below

pictures of pictures of you and the animal who watches

wet wings, hair reaching another direction's god

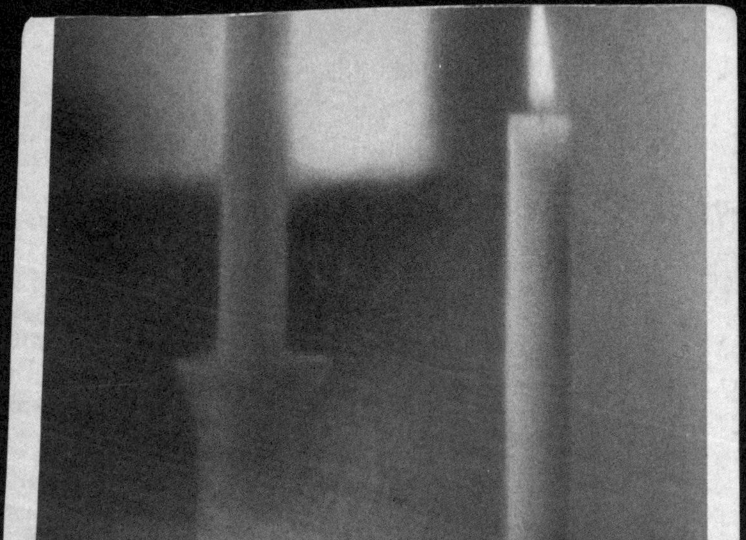

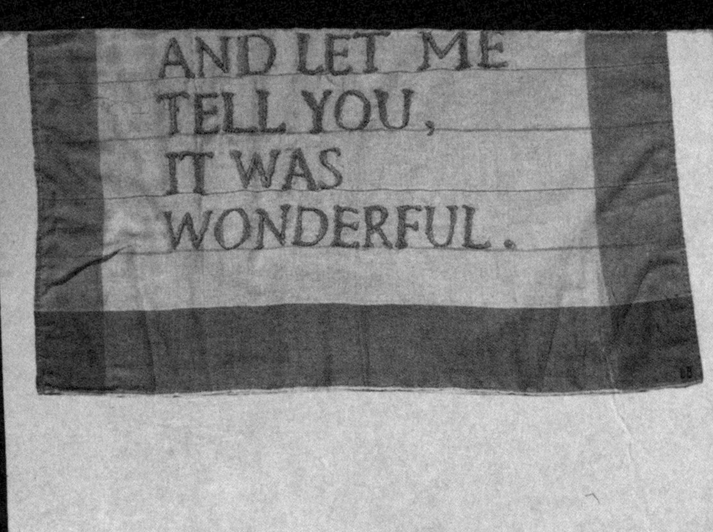
AND LET ME
TELL YOU,
IT WAS
WONDERFUL.

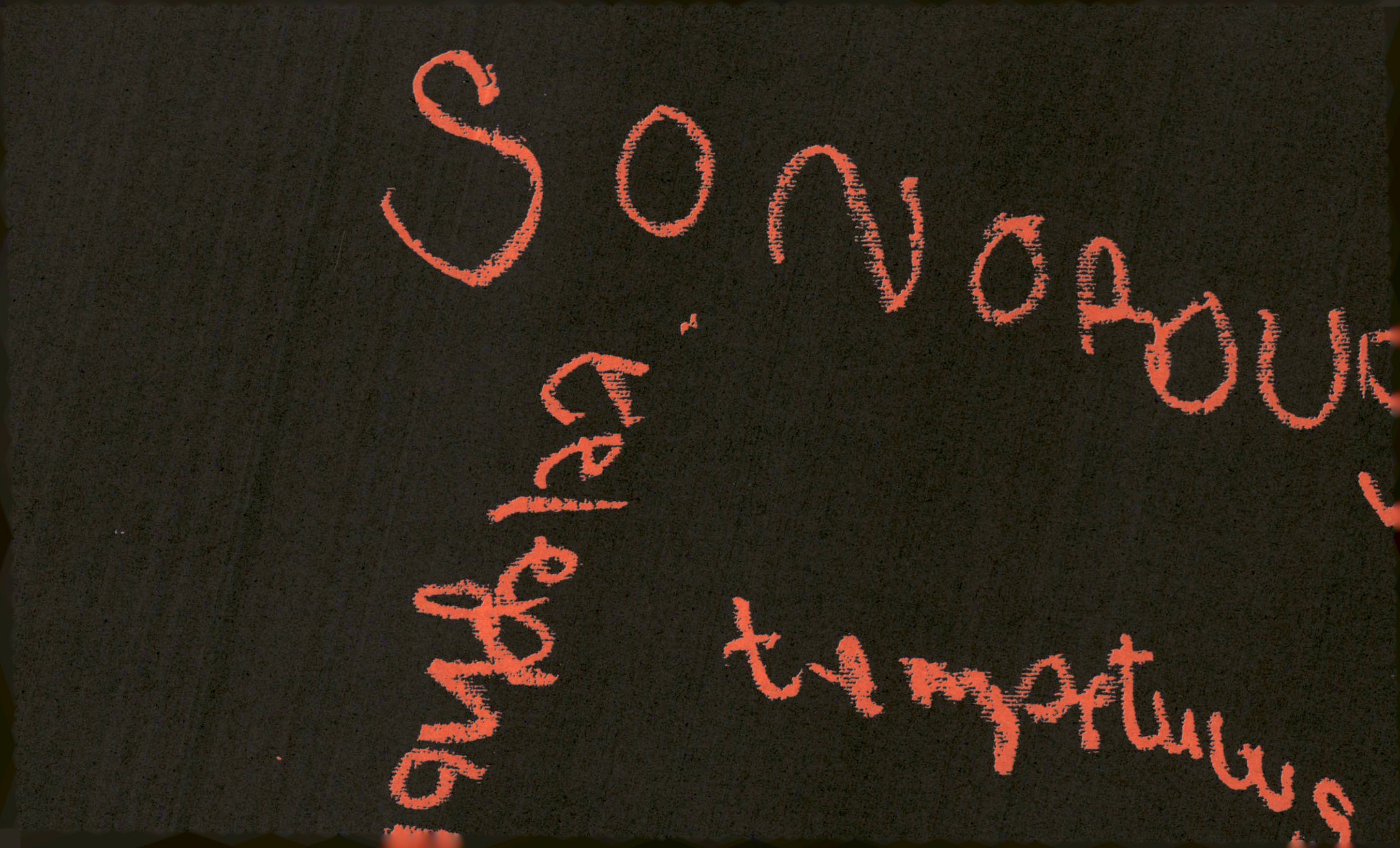

Sonorous
telephone

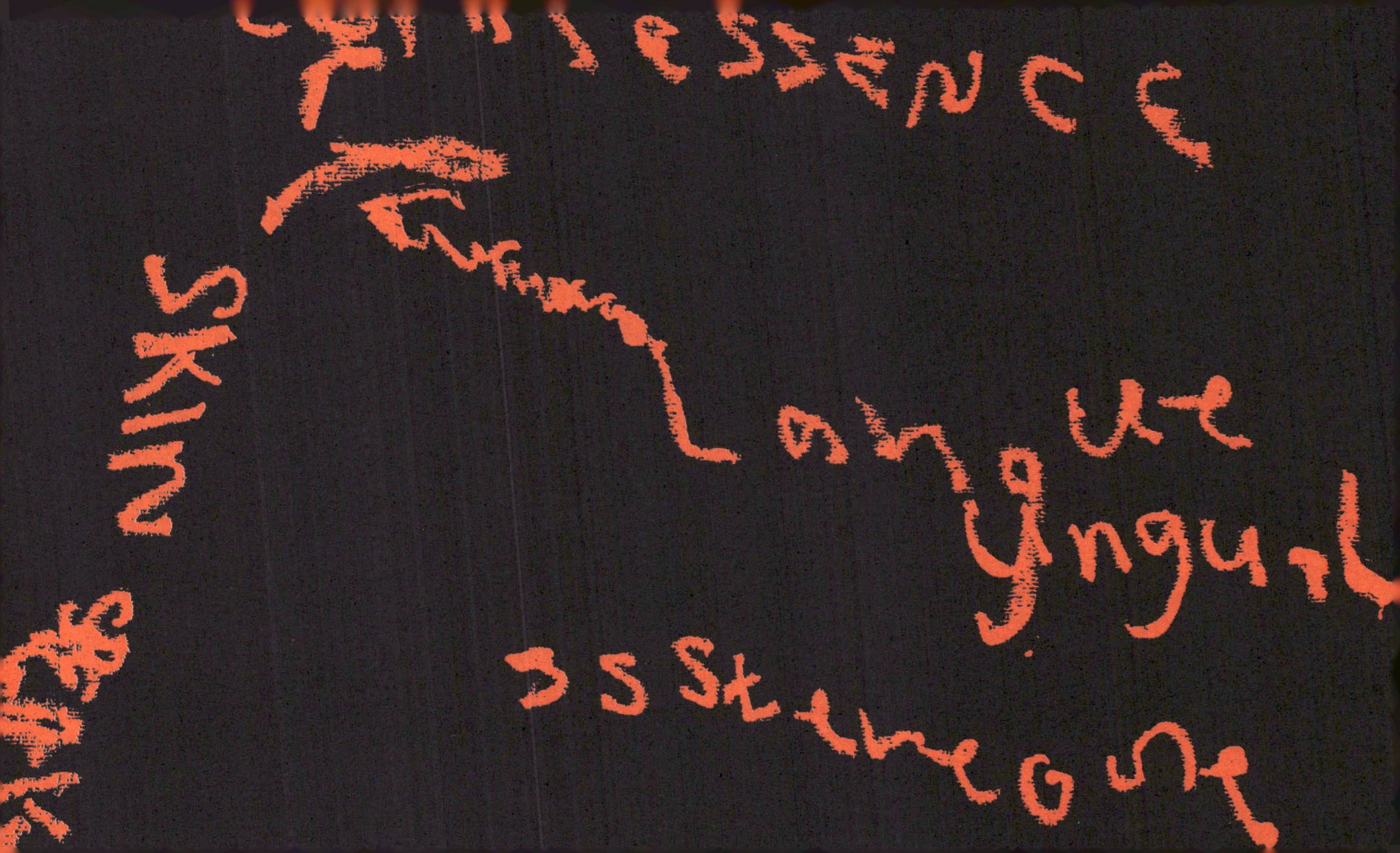
Longue
SKIN

speaker is a microphone

he said, *What if you were trying to describe red*
but all you had was blue and green?
a name is not boundless, it's binding

side by side
a 1992 tattoo of the sun
the year they found a third centaur in the dark
a woman asks me if i can read and i can't

titanium clip links to sky
a metal flower chamber with a baby t on a baby
an eagle on a seal
all the ridges outlined in snakes
a tiger with concrete teeth is the stairs
the floor your body

Tell me the story of all these things
beginning wherever you wish,
tell even us

the DMZ is the most preserved stretch of
nature in the world
all nature is second nature if we acknowledge
what we've already done

deface, as in to *mar the face of, to vandalize*, *without face*,
the mourning of someone you don't know
the mourning of someone you don't know
how to love
embroidered on a lotus leaf at night

you need to decide whether to tuck or not to tuck
spoiler alert: all the victims in all the units are fucking special,
But i'm a creep

when i was seven Changok gave me 100,000 KRW because it was his motorcycle and no one was sure if i would walk again. i came out of anesthesia and the surgeon said well, *she'll never be in Playboy* and gave me a red popsicle. the part of my cheek they sewed to my heel never really healed. two years later Changok rode the motorcycle across the 38th parallel crashing in North Korea. he woke up with a new face.

If you took a slice of the universe you should be able to read the whole universe in it, or at least that's what she told me a hologram is.

there is a newly printed 3D bust of Tutankhamun made from 2,000 CT body scans. topless eyes underlined in black, pouting gay face, shaved head. i had a crush on a 3,342-year-old teen goth.

finding the other side of the other side is not you
Korean theater has a genre where women play all the roles

for my brother's sixteenth birthday my mother asked me to jump out of a cake and sing *Billie Jean* in a bikini. i said but mom you know i'm... vegan, right? her brother was not dead yet

the grid lit up for you on the edge of the world
your negation our accident
you become an illusory light

eclipse
a cloth
a tiger

the first live performance of *Billie Jean* was the premiere of the moon walk. *Among the large headlines concerning Apollo this morning, there's one asking that you watch for a lovely girl with a big rabbit. An ancient legend says a beautiful Chinese girl called Chang-o has been living there for 4,000 years. It seems she was banished to the Moon because she stole the pill of immortality from her husband. You might also look for her companion, a large Chinese rabbit, who is easy to spot since he is always standing on his hind feet in the shade of a cinnamon tree. The name of the rabbit is not reported.*

the Korean shaman ritual is called a *Kut.* the word was Romanized with a K until the year 2000 when the Revised Romanization of Korean replaced the McCune–Reischauer system and it became *Gut* with a "g." in the *Gut* a shaman may embody the illness of her client or, wearing men's robes, will impersonate and make fun of the gods in a dance.

the bell is not rung to mark time but to break it
to shake the viscous container into its brilliant parts

when the men became shamans they identified with Confucianism and Buddhism
he didn't know a witch is a cliff and the fall from the cliff
as if we could stop the break we're being
when *the flower and seed are produced at the same time*

on Mount Inwangsan a fence is built in the cut between North and South
guards stationed at the peaks, a tourniquet on faith
no flag commemorates the sky, which didn't need you to see it
the body escapes through a key reduced to its essential parts
What time is it on the clock of the world?

scientists announced it was two minutes to midnight
fabricating only a quarter of a clock face for the presentation
the last time it was 1953
the year the war ended
the year the DMZ was made
the year no one knows if my mother was born until she became a
horse like Chiron's

god is a woman is i'm not sure
remember Poksun on the night shift at the Nike plant
i kept having that dream last summer of someone batting them out of
the stadium Air Force Ones flying
you said i liked manufactured things instead of handmade ones as if
there were no hands in a factory
fingerprints smudged from a stone we named after her

what you remember about me is that house cut you at the knees
the breathing roof of a person who was a thing waits at your window
someone, but not quite, offers a net

peel back the receiver to the socket
Let the sound enter from without
they landed double forever
no blame

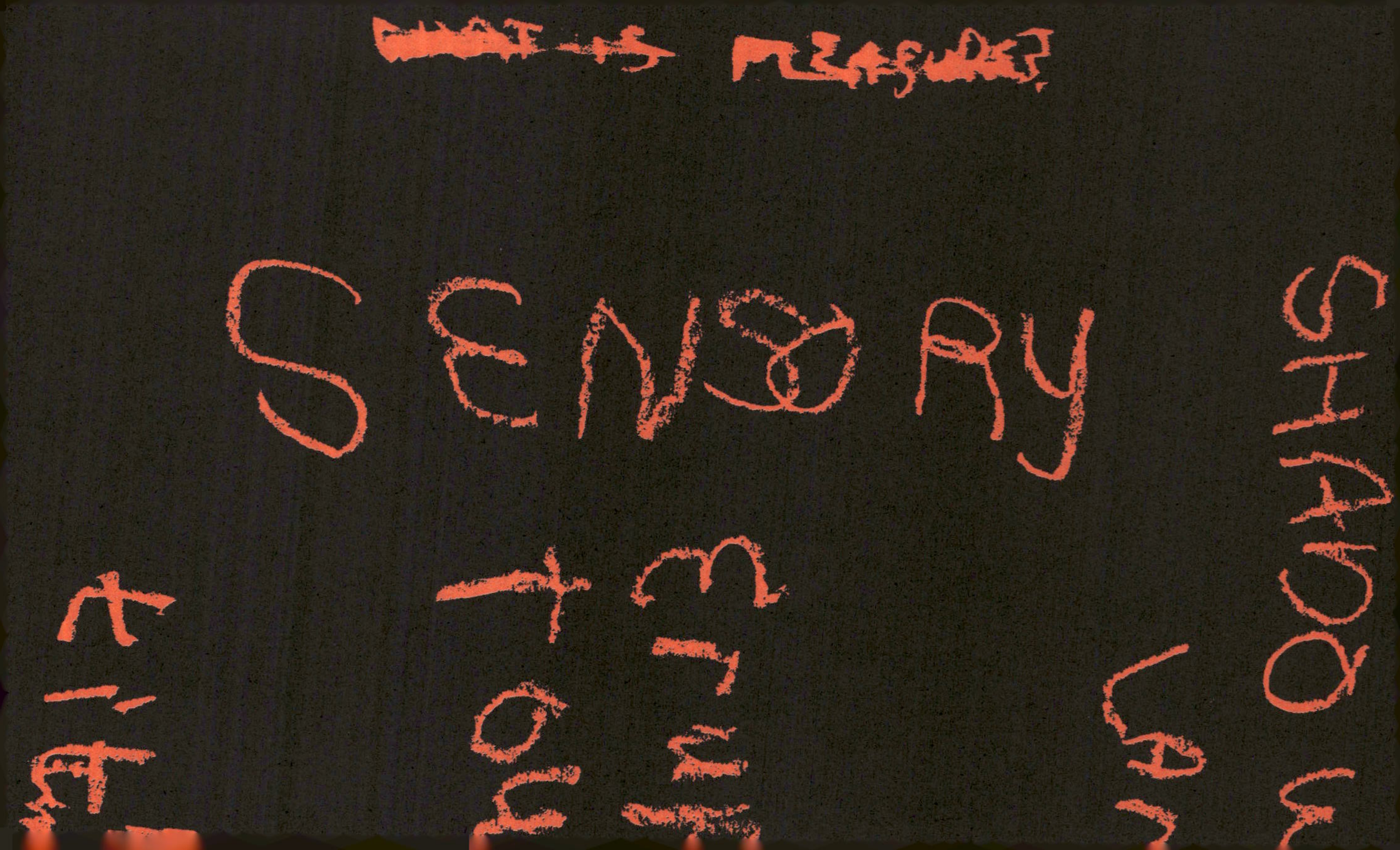
PLEASURE?
SENSORY
SHADOW

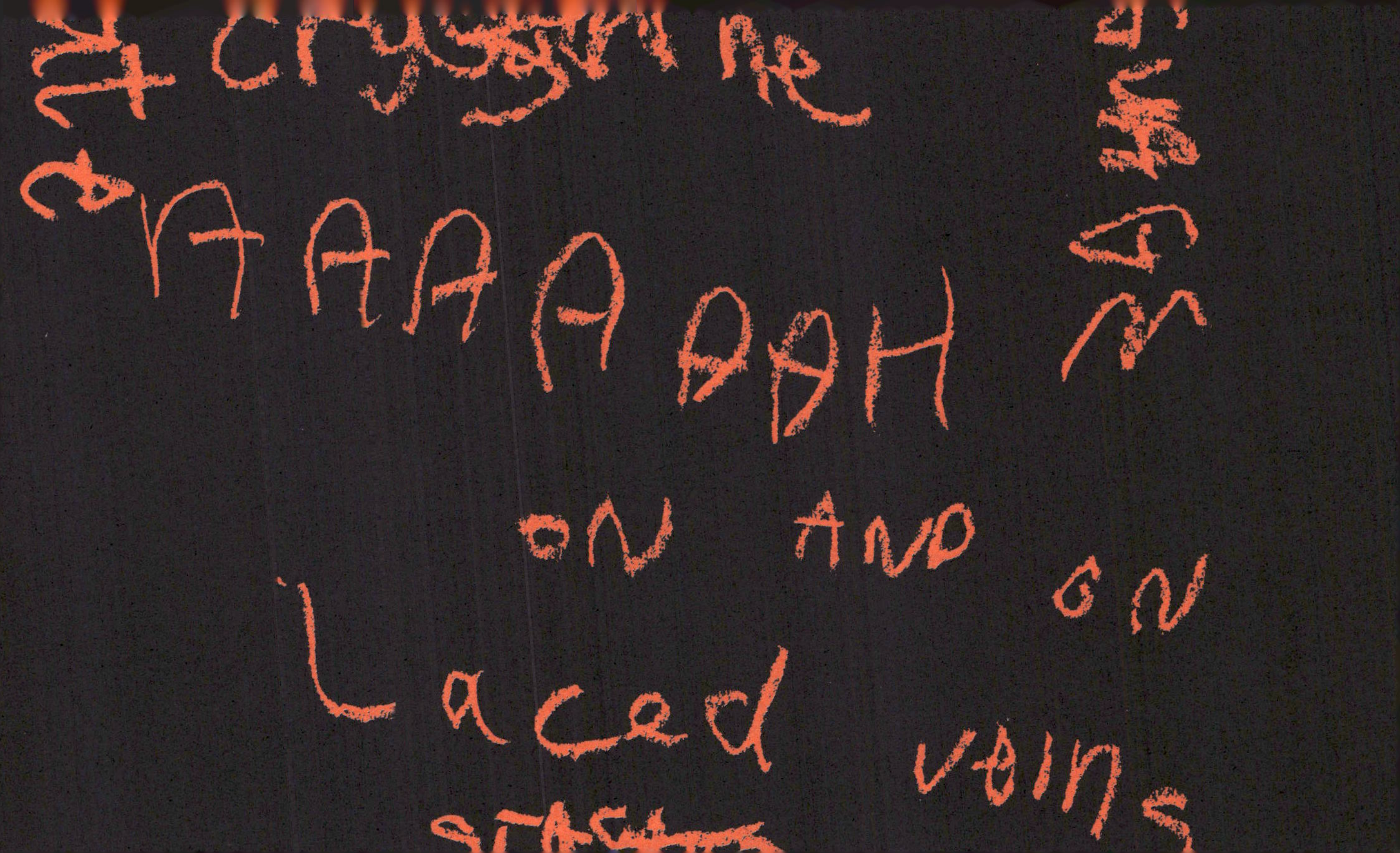

AAAAAAH
on and on
Laced veins

밤시각
Night Vision

on top
the gasoline slicked juice
your mirror
your excess
your absence
a proper noun
called you everywhere
but there are no corners on Earth

i will make your name
from all the stars in the dark

CD skipping into the next life

the wound in my belief in the material world

gone toward a hole
tongue open
taught me to draw a rose one petal at a time
my memory wants it to be a dozen roses rose
but i know it has a different face
Chemyon, saving face

as far as the eye can see let me go
last night a tiger balm
not still like a picture
like something you can take

he asked if she was a famous shaman
no one in our family even knows her name
i have no names
i have many names
what they mean when they say go home and that is nowhere

There's always tomorrow is old fashioned too
the Hindu mantra sounded just like the Korean words for
I don't know, baby, I don't know
the part i come back to because this time was our flesh
i know i said i promise in another language
i still mean it

when i asked if you would like my poems
i knew your cunt before we met
halftone hydrating essence
midnight arms a gate
water is never a prisoner
all the emojis of the earth
a gesture for an apology for the unspeakable

she said to stand on the knives brought her a softness
of the whispers
BB CC ZZ cream *sukk muri* dream
underskin tattoo
there was not one line but many
crossed
every wall lying down to lick itself
skinny dipping someone else's uniform

all the lakes last season's skies
all the women make it uncomfortable
the past on another rhythm
reverse tiger pose
rabbit all the stars back in the box
the bank makes your mother's name a secret
you make a shadow on the moon

show me everything you have to lose
now lose

i had to become an animal because we know they die
high heels to heaven
long sleeves to hell
Google translation of an ancient tone

at age four
between the piercing of my left and right ear
i went outside to say goodbye to the tree in front of the house
the rocks on the ground and the sky
i had a belief in animism but not futurity

you said
Remember forever when it happens.

you said
To make love, turn to page 121.
To die, turn to page 172.

HAN
NAH

What are you affiliated with?

a drugstore box marked *Secret Hole*
a shimmering sticker on real life
a hand on a door that hadn't been made yet
Ultraviolet hologram
contraband
the night is a paywall every other second
but in between it's free
how to give the proper respect to someone
you put inside a cage of your own learning
as if the humane choice meant something benign
a round note
sonar? heartbeat
the blush turns blue
all its veins waving against the screaming day
fluorescent night burns through the blinds

V-line
the grid goes flaccid
every part of the room my body
floor body
corner body
ceiling body
stop body
go body

water catches net
rock beats human

we came from another time
we came to another time

we called you tiger
because it was as big a name as you didn't have
we used your version of the world because it was invisible

2020/01/19
09:51:02

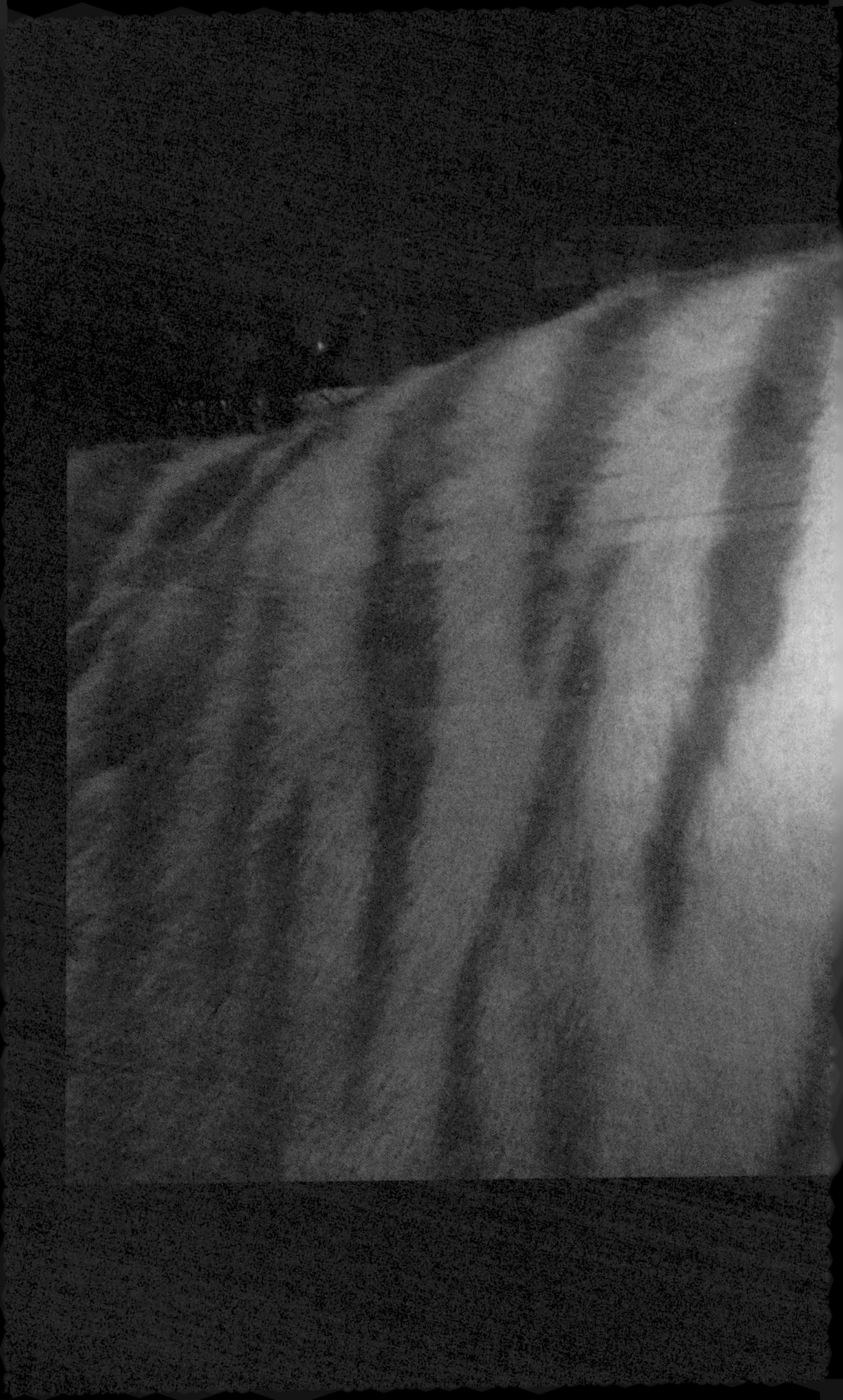

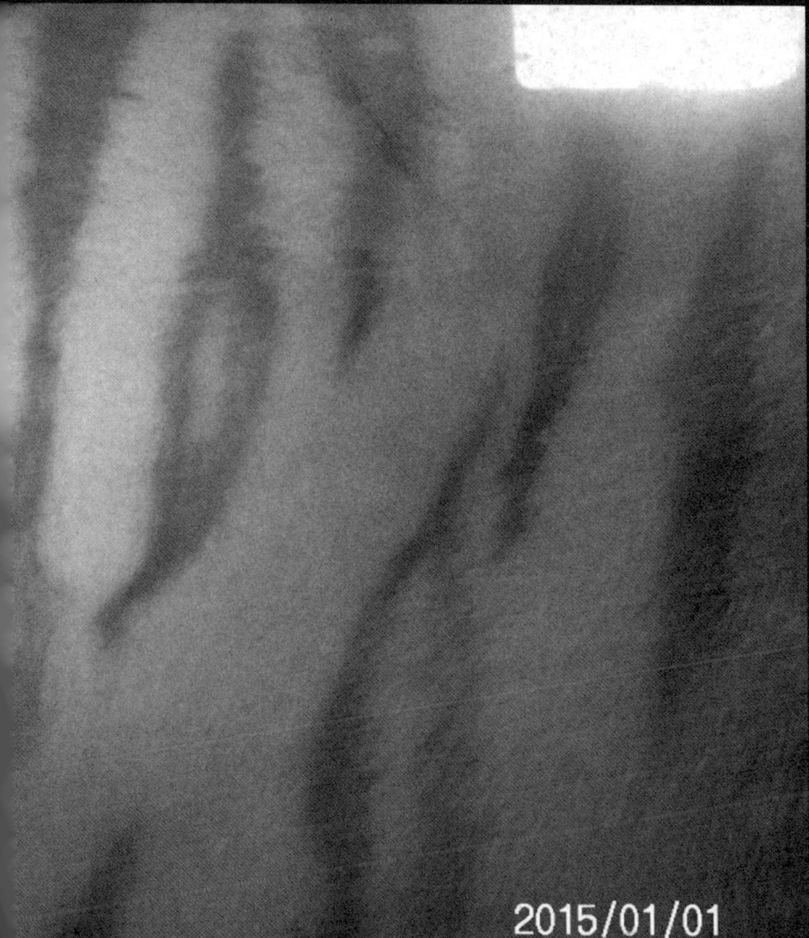

2015/01/01
00:09:48

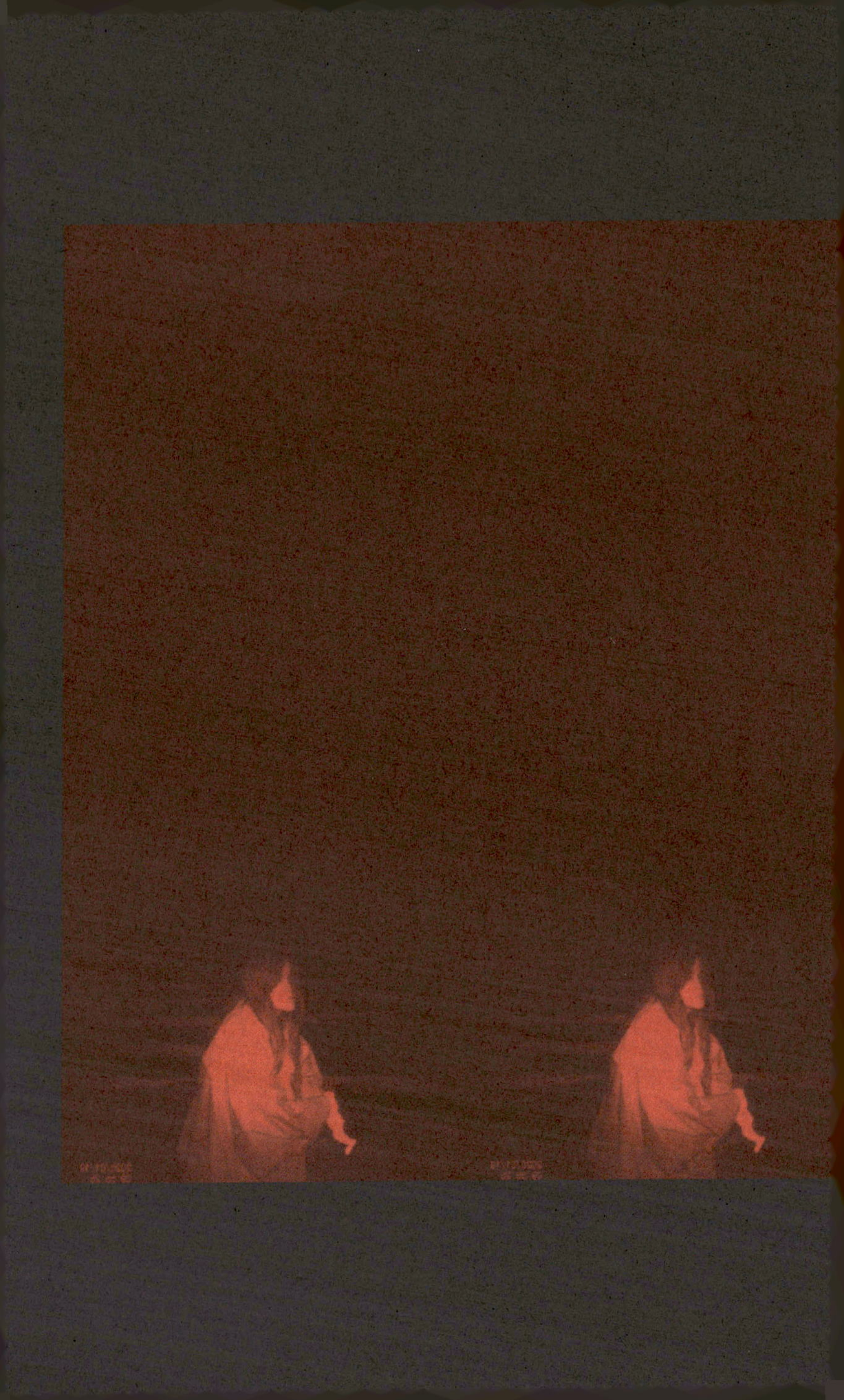

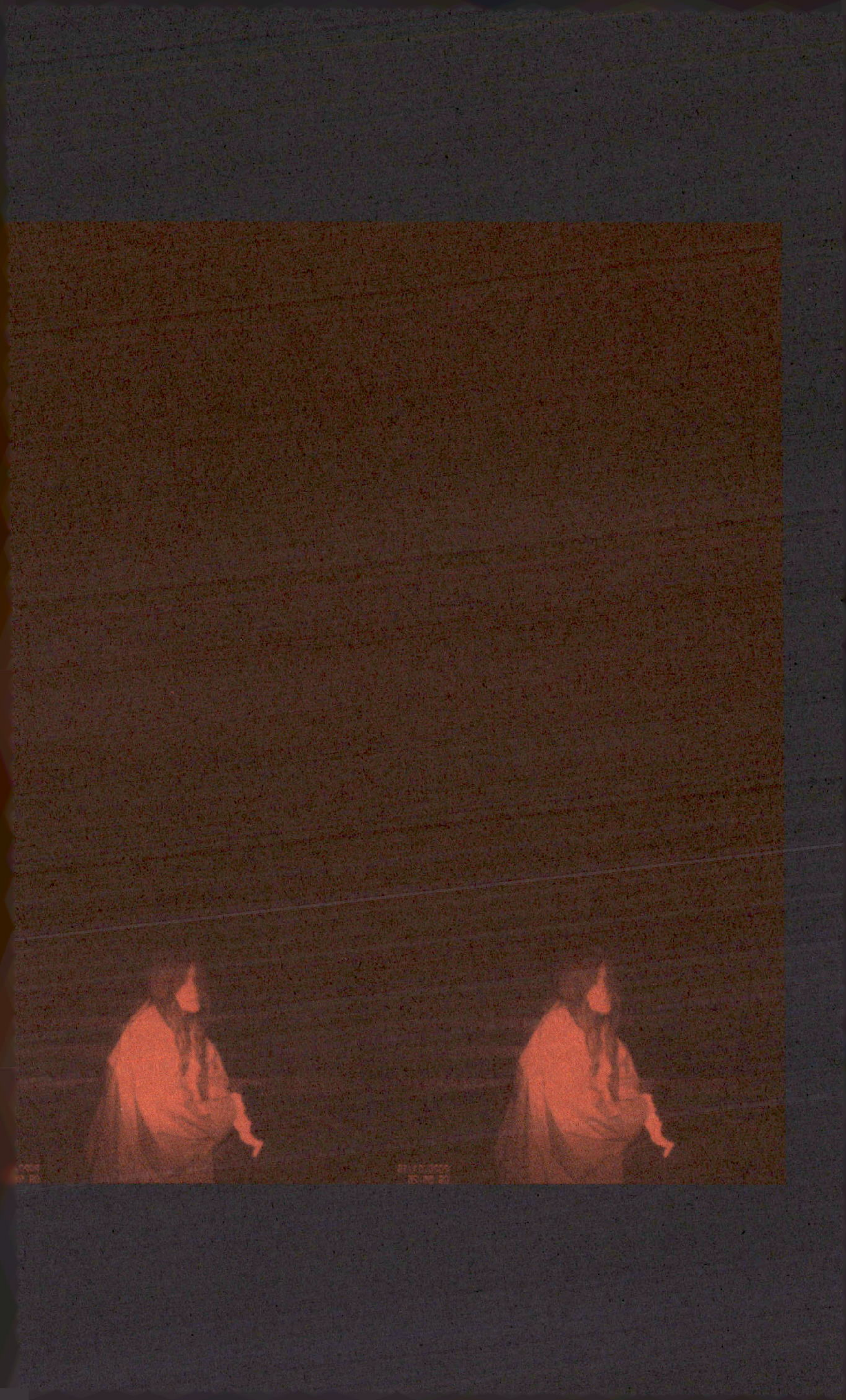

2020/01/19
09:48:38

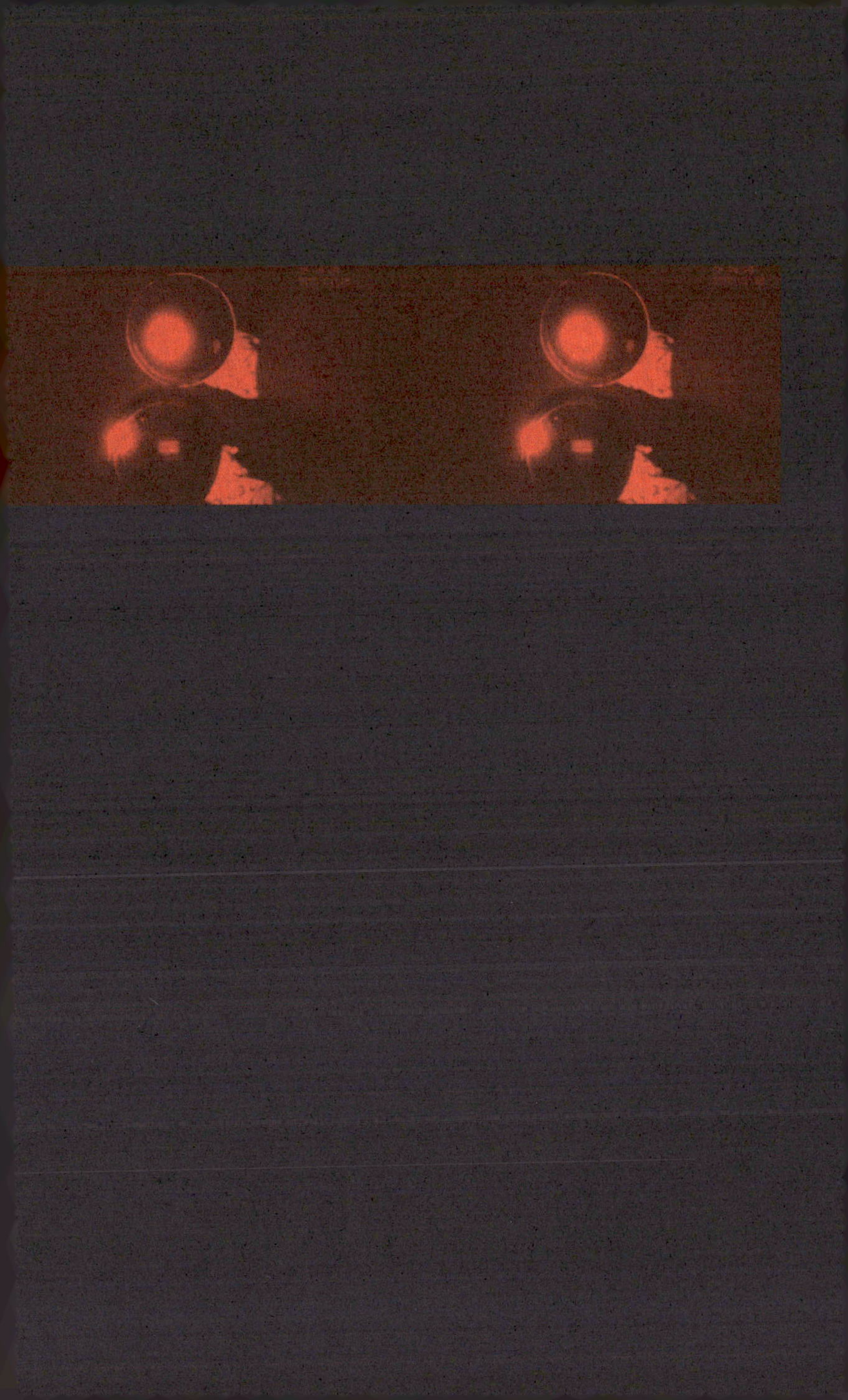

terra
STUTTER AGAIN AND
AGAIN
SEER SEAR
EAR

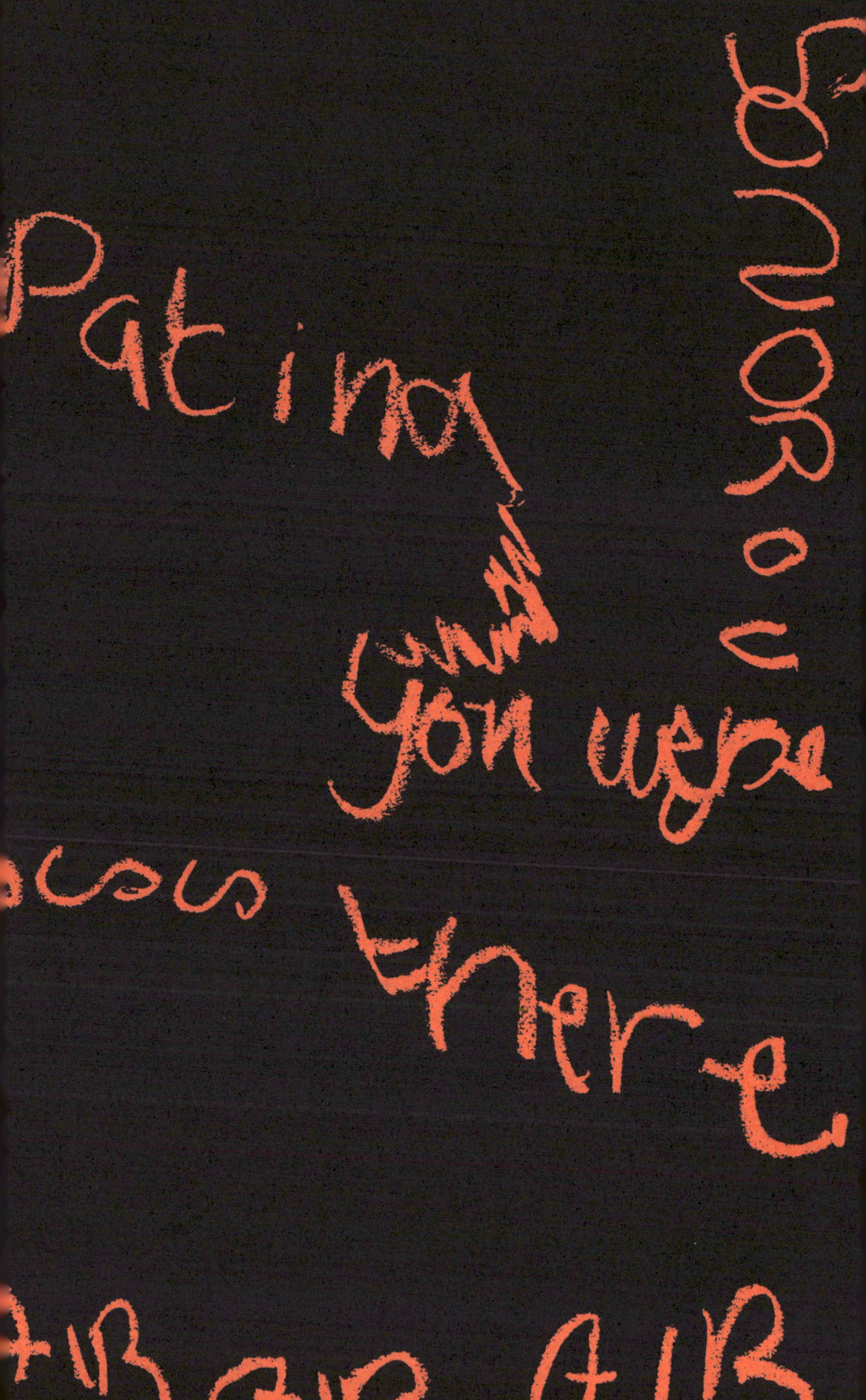
you were
there

Measuring with a bent ruler

All but the third Sunday of each month, I would walk in and find all kinds of juice on sale. Not to buy, but stand next to.
—Renee Gladman

on one side of the cup in a gold leaf with holes shot through the name NANCY in all caps. on the other side someone had painted a picture of Bambi. K said, *Oh, you picked the good cup.*

Gon is assigned to me and he starts by saying *I understand that you're a feminist but I wonder if also no one can tell.* it's true, i don't believe in equality. Paridegi doesn't go to the underworld to get the elixir of life to get the elixir of life.

i don't make the video. i turn on the camera which you can't really be sure of because there is no screen and only later i watch. it's hard to let it do what it wants because i keep trying to see what it is: breaking. i wake from the dream about the giant earring back feeling that i need to make the object, but why? months later i spot the small metal clasp on the floor and reach for my ear: the moment you know you've lost something. i ask Nayop for the first time, what is it like when the voices speak to you? and she says, *There is a window that flickers with a pattern of light.* i don't remember this until later but of course it's how the video is shown, at the edge of everything.

If no one is around you say baby I love you.
—Destiny's Child

Pehlki got her name from the Dalai Lama. for a long time i thought it was Peggy and how it was cute that he called her that. eventually Young Joo had to spell it for me. when we met, she said, *Your name is so beautiful—Mira, my mirror. I see myself in you. You know Mira means mummy, like someone dead.*

K was also Asian and White and said, *Maybe from the violent collision, our bodies could be some kind of peace.* benevolent generalizations on mixed-race heteronormative reproduction are boring partly because the leading cause of death in women is men. the malevolence of desire makes it sharp, but also round, and when only one-sided, flat. K knew this, so i didn't think about the family, but about my body as witness, receipt.

The unreachability of some things can be affective; it can even put other worlds within reach.
—Sara Ahmed

Laura told me that i needed to go to a waterfall to receive a download and that i needed to go with Saewon. she had not seen the documentary about the shaman who trained with one, trying every day to sing louder than the crash. Saewon texted that Grace left a crystal for her in a waterfall in Jeju. so that narrowed it down. when we got to the first waterfall, there was a vertical screen showing a 1-minute loop of footage of the waterfall displayed in a small house in the woods where you could leave notes. it hadn't rained in a while and there wasn't enough water to see it outside. a woman at the fruit stand nearby also showed us a video on her phone from a couple months before. these images were kind of tender because they were such small containers. at the next waterfall, there were lots of people, there was a line for selfies, and for 10,000 KRW you could borrow a traditional wedding headdress for your picture. the small nudity of trying to catch something in your hand. we sat at the water's edge and started singing a single note. we'd been doing this a lot, i don't know how it started. (now i remember the secret Baul singing lessons Samita gave me in the basement last summer, sinking through the nine gates of the body. she said, *Because I know death is in your world.)* i tried to look at the fall not like a picture, something still that you can take, but like falling. water catches net. if you follow a drop from the top all the way to the bottom again and again and then you look away, everything you see starts to move, the people are shaken off the shore, the wooden platform curls up. rock beats human. i thought it would be more like language, i didn't know if i was doing it right. we found a sculpture nearby and laid our hands on this golden part of it. someone came up to us and asked if the sculpture was making the sound. after Young Joo told her it was us, she asked if she could touch it too. early in the trip i wished we could dance in one of the mini trucks driving around Jeju because of the girl who thought i was from where Björk is from, and then we saw one in the parking lot. after dancing in it a while we noticed someone standing there silently watching us. she asked what we were affiliated with. we had recently made a word for vagina since there isn't one we could think of in Korean that was specific and not awful. we loosely based it on the void and Saewon's recurring mispronunciation of the word for rainbow.

Q: 우리는 누구와 제휴 했는가?
Q: 무 재 ...우리가 생각해 낸 단어가 뭐야?
Q: 무 재 기?

she smiled and stood there with us for a long time and then asked if she could have her truck back. after driving away, she returned to the parking lot to see if we wanted to come home with her. on the final day in Jeju, Nayop called and said, *I was just watching videos of waterfalls on the Catholic channel and thought of you.* i hadn't told her where i was or what i was doing. why did waterfalls make you think of me? *Because it's your name.* what's my name? *I named you after the Chinese word for waterfall, don't you remember? I told you when you were eleven.* i felt bad then for cutting my name in two like the Chinese word for unicorn because i stopped being a woman eighteen years ago. i tried to tell her where i was and what i was doing but that is not what Nayop likes to talk about. *It's time for you to understand the energy of things. I'm sure they teach you this in art school, that everything has a different energy, like stones but also pictures or whatever.* no, they didn't teach me that. *Well, everything has it and you have it and you need to pay attention to it. You need to make a choice.* about what? *About what you want.*

What do you want to be when you die? I'm going to be something that has no borders.
—Kim Hyesoon

Eliza said it would be good to learn about dismemberment. Laura said to practice by watching tiger videos. Ariana said the tiger was the part of me that shines. and Pil said i was trying to find the tiger's spirit so i had to pray every day and go to a mountain. mostly i would put Tiger Balm on my face, crawl and meditate for the six minutes it took to steep tea in my studio, which was on a tall landfill that had been turned into a forest. during the last week in Seoul, a message came: *IF YOU TAKE YOUR CAMERA TO THE BORDER YOU CAN CROSS.* i had only been watching the break, i hadn't thought to use it. on the bus to the DMZ with the British teens who took sexy photos at all the stops, i let *Caliban and the Witch* open, a page about animality and shapeshifting. thankfully, Leire had already wanted to go and agreed to hold my camera. we arrived at the observatory on Mount Dora, the closest civilian point along one of the most guarded military borders in the world. i got on the ground and asked Leire to face me and then try to face North Korea. i hoped it would break in the right spot. after i started walking on my hands, our tour guide, nervous, kneeled down to me and whispered, *Tell me you have lost something. Tell me you are looking for something.*

우리가 다 있어
우리가 다 이뻐
우리가 아니야

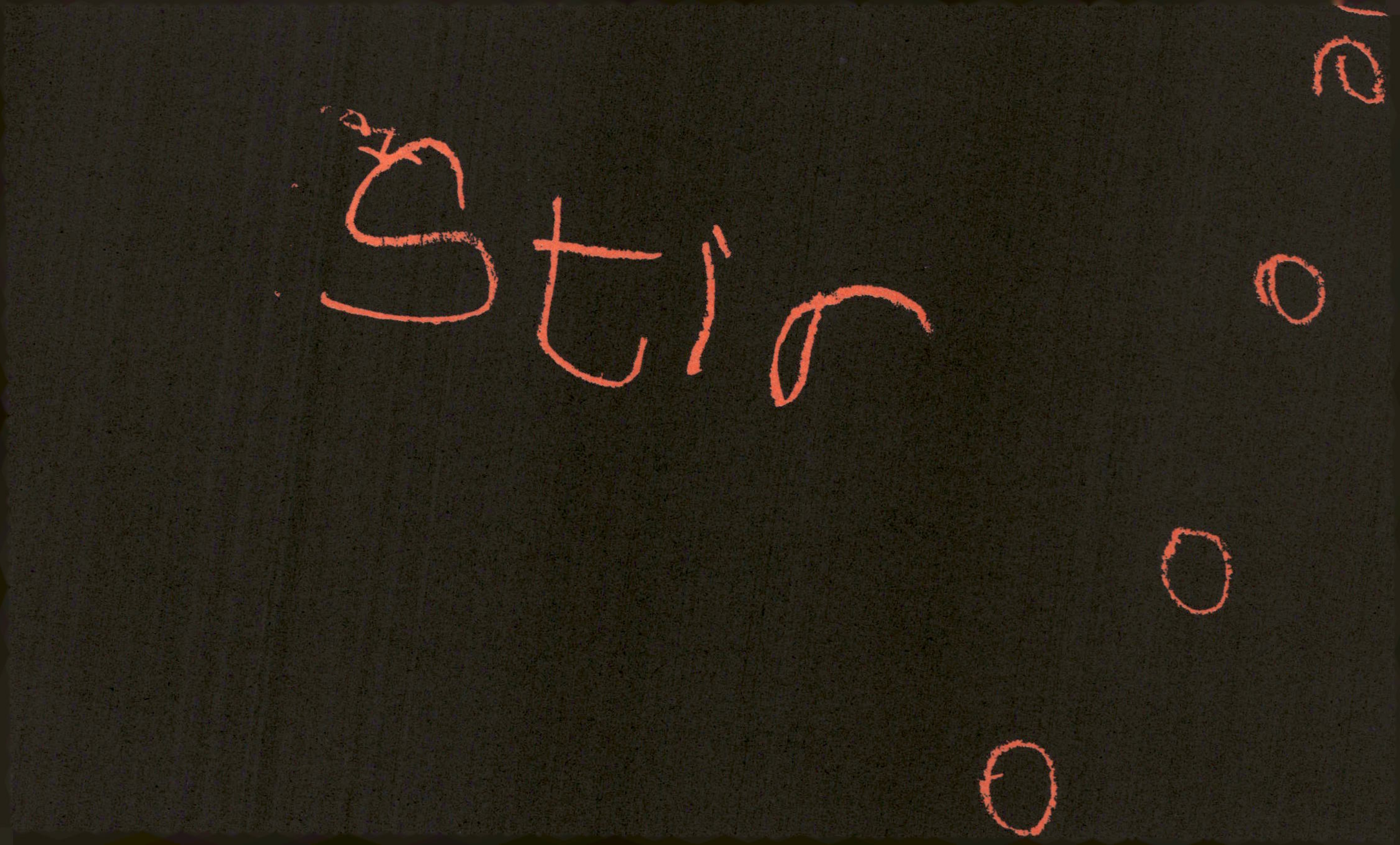
Stir

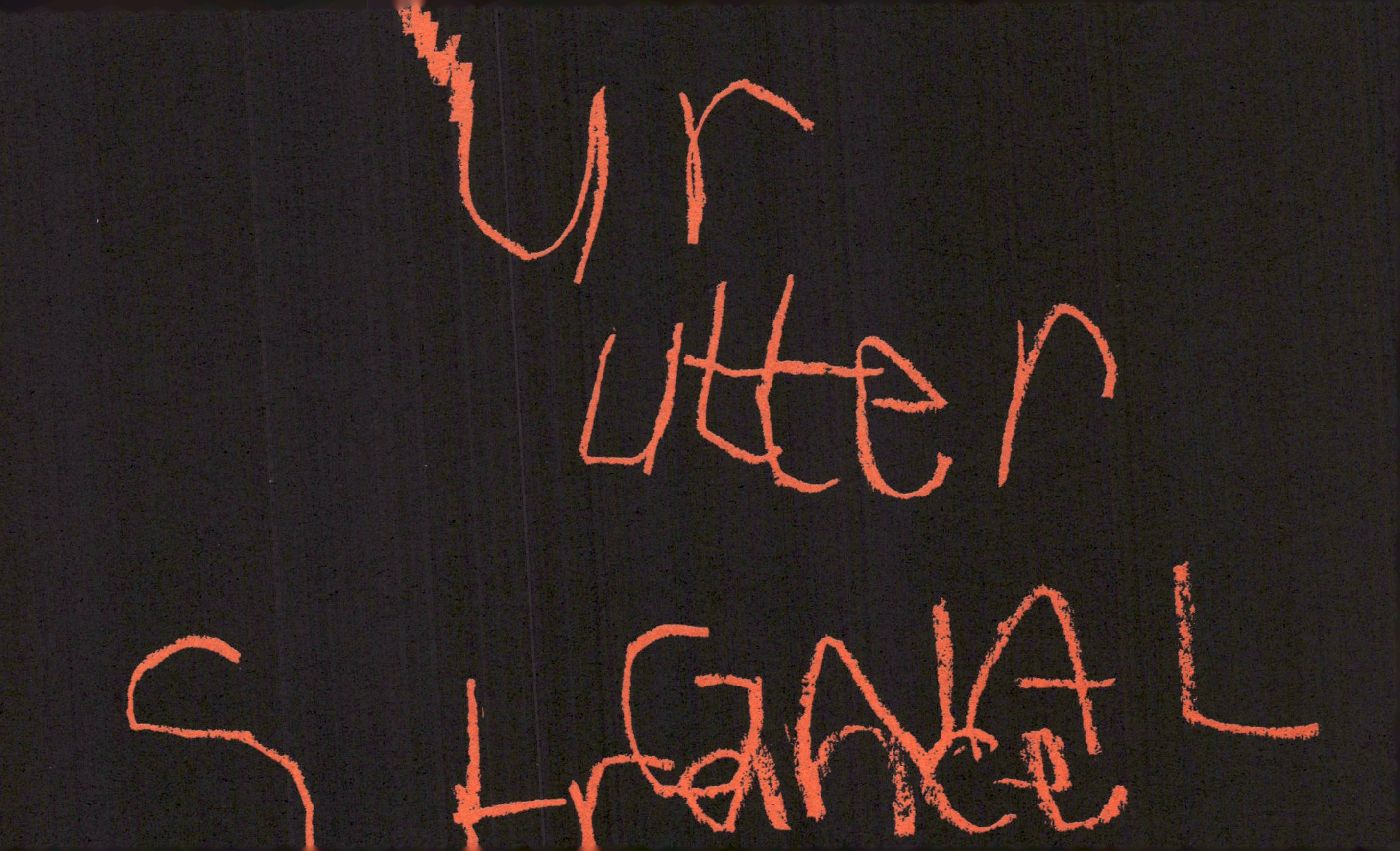
Ur
utter

The Book of Fixed Stars.

cryotype

A

Channel 1/ Left front / South Li Fire ☲

Illumination, brilliance. Add Water elements for flow.
Secrets, memories.

Channel 2/ Right front / Southeast Zun Wind ☴

Reflection, penetrating. Add Water elements for flow.
Dreams, poetry, the unknown.

B

Channel 1/ Left back / Northwest Q'ian Heaven ☰

Ask questions, receive feedback and knowledge from the past.
Strength through adaptability.

Channel 2/ Right back / North Kan Water ☵

Confined activity. Add Wood elements for expansion.
New, potential energy, green, tiger.

B
the passed-down body was endless
not a genetic
but an adaptive suite
she didn't know if it was early heaven
or later heaven
maybe there was a middle

A
bells all night but who rings them
the room was small and turned like they call a woman
every sky in your pocket
eyes doubled up so there was a set for god
the slippery sex that swelled from thousands of x-rays

B
the pet psychic said the tigers live in a state of constant
forgiveness
not a cup but when it's spilled over past your life
they didn't need me to find them
they were not afraid

A
contrapunctual cord
between heaven and earth
the third skin
am i your last chance or are you mine?

B

i dusted my ear in crystal and pressed up against the glass
all of us outside
covered in phones
in jeans
you gave me a name
not like a word but like the color green
like a heart

A

all my love a comet in the ring
we will place our things around the edges

B

DREAM 06/18/2019 *I AM EVERY DROP OF WATER.*

she drew the lines of a holographic universe we were all already touching through

A

no longer your own accuser

B

the page they place my receipt in Ocean's book that reads
The name tiger had become a bridge
the postcard i got of Yayoi Kusama on a bridge with a banner that reads *SELF-OBLITERATION*
everyone covered in dots, atomized

A

When were you born?

B

September 19, 1982

When were you born?

A

December 20, 1982

B

I was older than I should have been

I remember the cat more than I remember her

They thought I was some other kind of thing

Something about the air something about everything even the milk tastes different

A

In the house?

B

No, in Thailand. Do you remember the smells?

A

i didn't like the taste of the orange juice. it came from a can,
and i thought the juice tasted like the can. then, last year,
i had a special orange grown on Jeju and it tasted like metal.
it's what made it special all along.

on the plane the woman next to me was sobbing at her small
screen watching *Night at the Museum* which has Rami
Malek playing an ancient Egyptian pharaoh in the Museum
of Natural History while my screen showed him as Freddie
Mercury singing *Radio Ga Ga*, who lived on in namesake
as a star who was born

i found in my notebook the word *contrapunctual* which means
something like a song played against the song that's playing

DREAM 07/09/2019 *I PAINTED A PICTURE. IT WAS OF
THE EARTH BUT ALSO OF ME.*

DREAM 03/18/2019 *I'M IN HAYDEN'S PLAY. I'M HAYDEN.
HER NEIGHBOR ASKS ME WHAT I'M DOING WITH MY
LIFE. AND I SAY I'M OLDER THAN I LOOK. IN THE
MIRROR I HEAR HIM DESCRIBING ME LIKE A SECURITY
GUARD.*

B

guard is interchanged with the word "observe" in Greek
translations of ancient Babylonian astronomy texts
as if every look was behind glass

A

DREAM 07/17/2019 *YOU PUT THE WORD ENTER AT THE EDGE OF EVERYTHING.*

B

as if every look was a promise

A

DREAM 08/18/2019 *I AM THE PARTICLE. MY WHOLE BODY IS IT.*

B

A. Turiyasangitananda Coltrane gave Shaam his name
the blue at the center of a monsoon
Krishna's skin
the void
he said *ohm* was symbolized by the number four
for wake, sleep, dream, with the fourth letter as silence
Mansin, a Korean word for shaman, means ten thousand
spirits
as in to be in conversation with
in Chinese the ten thousand things refers to the infinite

A

making up pictures for holes at night
Stars, they're just like us

A
we met once in the summer after not living there anymore
Brooke was the other half-girl in a small town
we met again when i inherited the chinoiserie

B
Grace told me Basquiat was in MoMA pouring water across the gallery floors. she said some spells you do in plain sight so no one notices.

while at Tut a half-girl in a Basquiat t-shirt walked in front of my camera so i followed her. there was nowhere to stand except down at his feet. he had two golden thong sandals with large bows and plated gold fingers for each finger, toe for toe. *I know you and I know your names.*

In the case of a black hole, the insight was that the informational content of all the objects that have fallen into the hole might be entirely contained in surface fluctuations of the event horizon.

A
electric outline
rearranging the sensation
bird samples loop
wishing on our fossilized tail
unwrapping the drink we order for the world
Schrödinger's pussy pissing in the corner of my being
crow shitting on a fake sign of a sign is a sign anointed
to mark the beginning of the end of the beginning and the end

like a lollipop should be licked
you said Prada meant prairie
Each other doesn't make any sense
i bought the purse from a woman at the market in Seoul
she only had one
an original '90s fake from the original sweatshop of the world
diamond gates every side of the jewel a blade
Earth
a question with no equal
all broken lines

do not forget the rose
the secret is under it

B
The punctum can be ill-bred.

you asked if they were knight shoes
moving like a letter
left at the door

the Crux was originally part of Chiron's foot
an intersection

A
gutted
kutted
broke

the wound dilated
its glossy mouth drums a round note
a friendship bracelet on a door handle
a tunnel tongued across years
a chronic life cycle
sky learned on a far channel
Stars, they're just like us

B
It is ontologically indeterminate which slit the electron
is going through because the slit is distributed not in space
but in time.

Tutankhamun's left foot was twisted
so his sole didn't touch the ground
the article said facetiously to put his hips in our porn folder
but i'm already in you

A black hole can only be measured with non-visual tools
including infrared heat and radio

A
coming out of anesthesia, the doctor said
She'll never be in Playboy
and asked do you want red or orange?
red or orange?

an interstellar elegy, employee of the month

B

Monument Eternal begins with Turiyasangitananda describing the atom as the father, the son, and the holy ghost; nothing can ever truly be destroyed. it ends with a description of her past life as shown to her by god: in ancient Egypt she was Ptolemy III.

in 150 Ptolemy wrote *The Almagest* in Greek.

in 964 Abd al-Rahman al-Sufi translated it into Arabic, added the Andromeda Galaxy, and made the first drawings of the constellations. *The Book of Fixed Stars* had mirror images of each constellation with one view from below and another from above. Chiron with brown skin and blue legs scattered with gold holes.

A

etching out the edges of an X
our gathered ego's earrings
the Earth a supporting actress in a drama
never won never one
shot on location
a snake in snakeskin pants
a crystal with your job on it
a tree cut into a chair that was your throat
a mesh eclipse
of trust proportion
of night in sun

violence parted on the stage begins the play
absence was the theater
we would all be going home

when we got back to the house there was a memorial
the floral wreath said *best friend*
we wondered if this was an animal
time in a lanyard of skins
standing prone under the inumbrated holiday
the dark scalloped your face out on a neon world
sleeping in a living room
shedding its walls
you're not like a painting but like something painted
i crossed your legs
the body weaves a hole
corona discharge

> B
> Hanuman—the flying monkey god, cursed to not remember who he is
> Hahnemann—founder of homeopathy
> the stronger the dilution the stronger the dose
> every piece of the hologram contains the picture
> every piece of the body contains the DNA

A
when i whispered your name onto the concrete
all ghosts concomitant undulating under god's green light
not enough hands for a circle

out of sight
out of mind
psychic spit
a pause in a room that hadn't been built

DREAM 08/22/2019 *THE EARTH WAS AN EXACT REFLECTION OF SOMETHING ELSE HANGING ON ONE HINGE. WE HAD TO LOVE BOTH BECAUSE THEY WERE PART OF THE SAME THING.*

when i first saw you
you had almost no discernible features
i could make you out from a great distance only
you followed me or i followed you
around a place no one believed in
just to test how tight the shape was we made
not the edge of the world, the edge of myself
kissing another version as it passes by

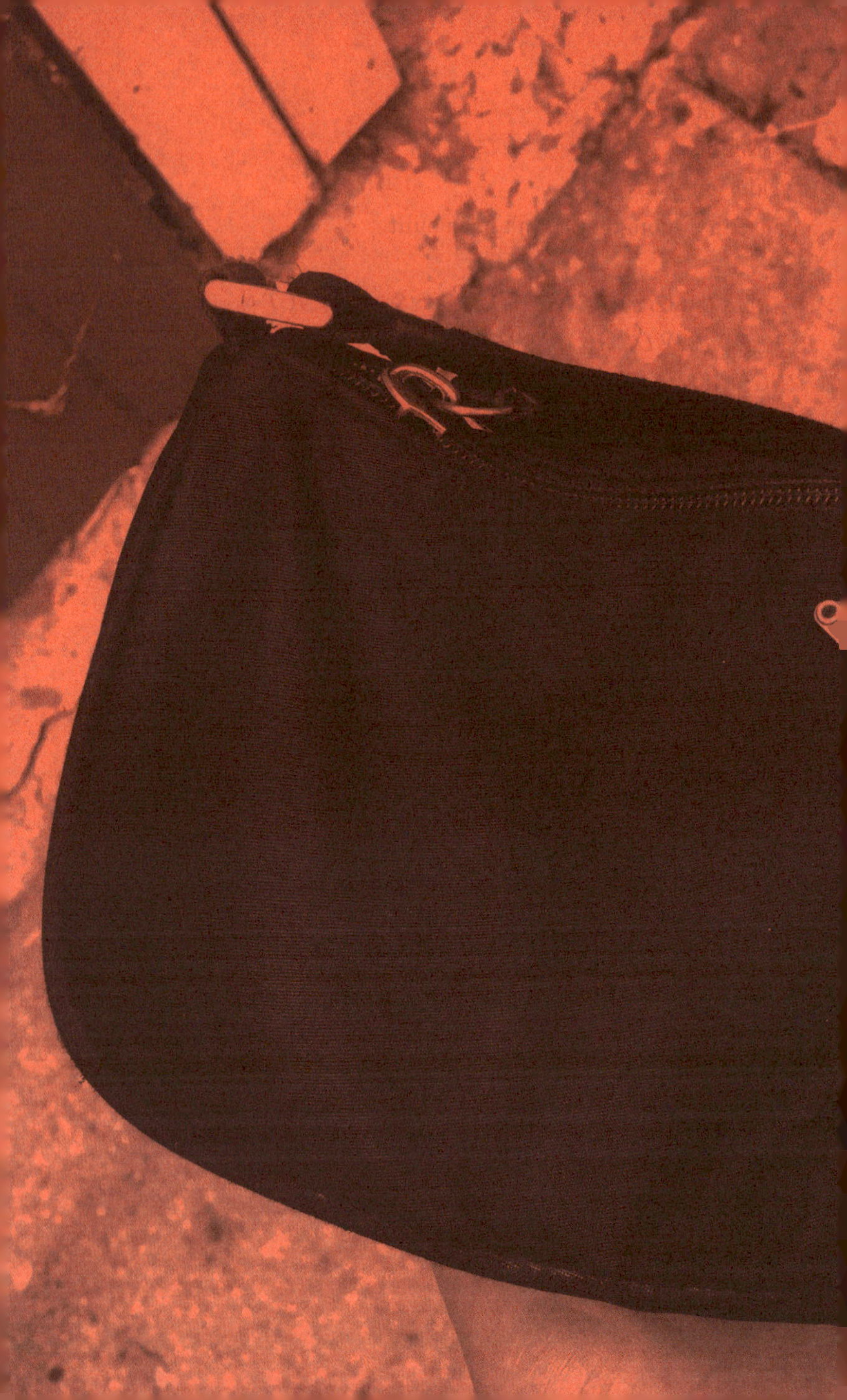

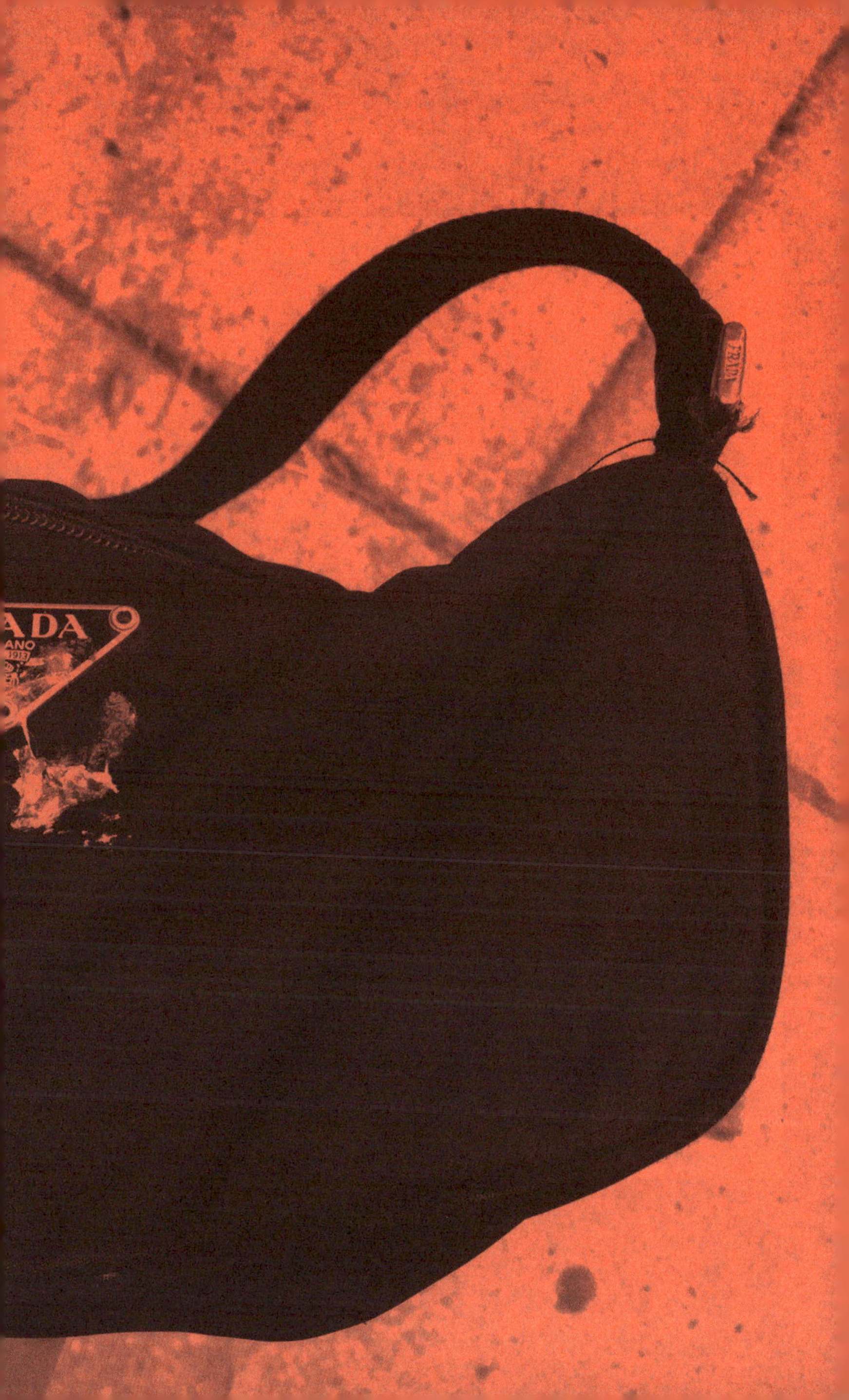
PRADA

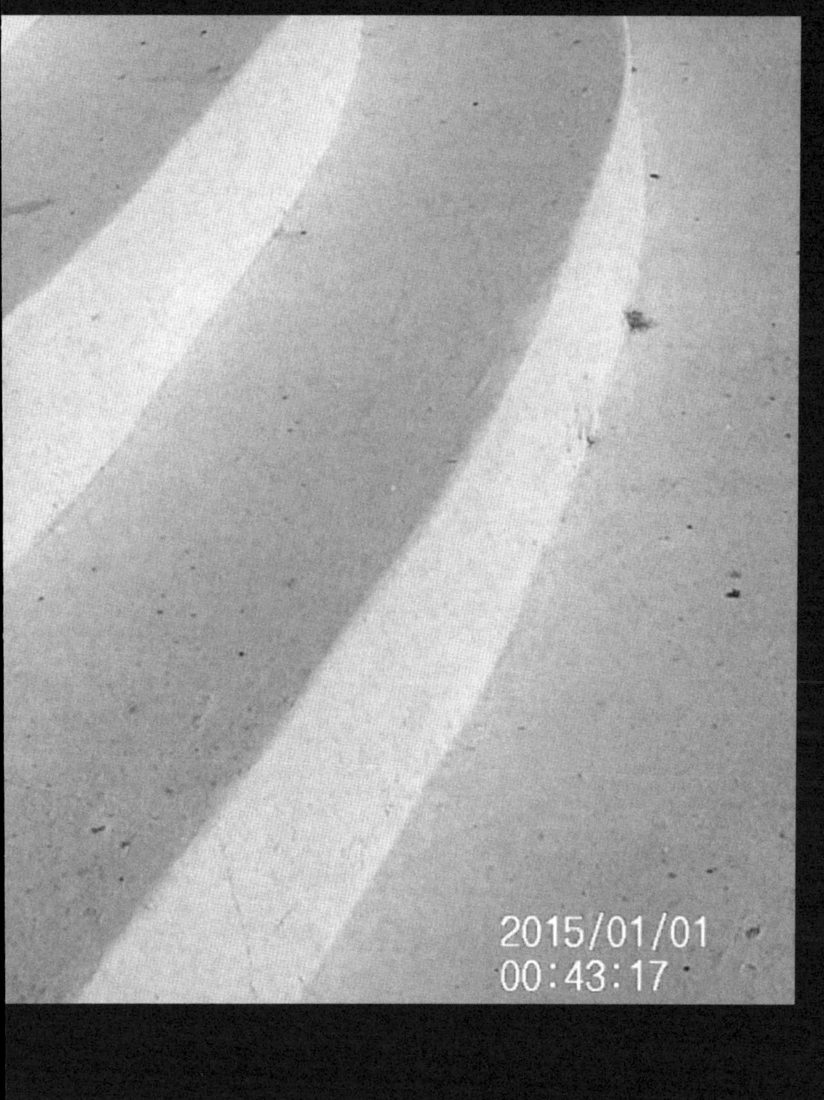
2015/01/01
00:43:17

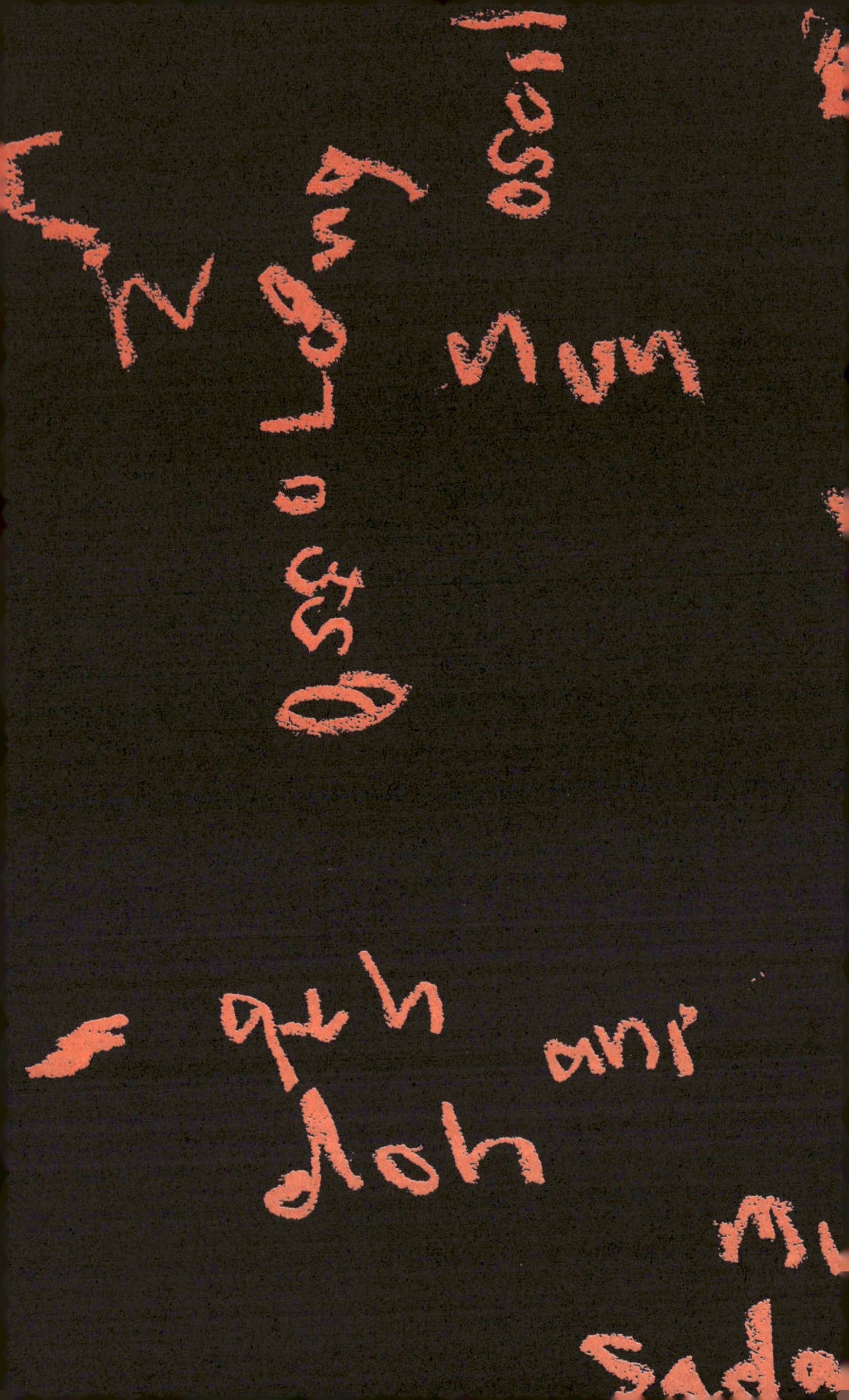

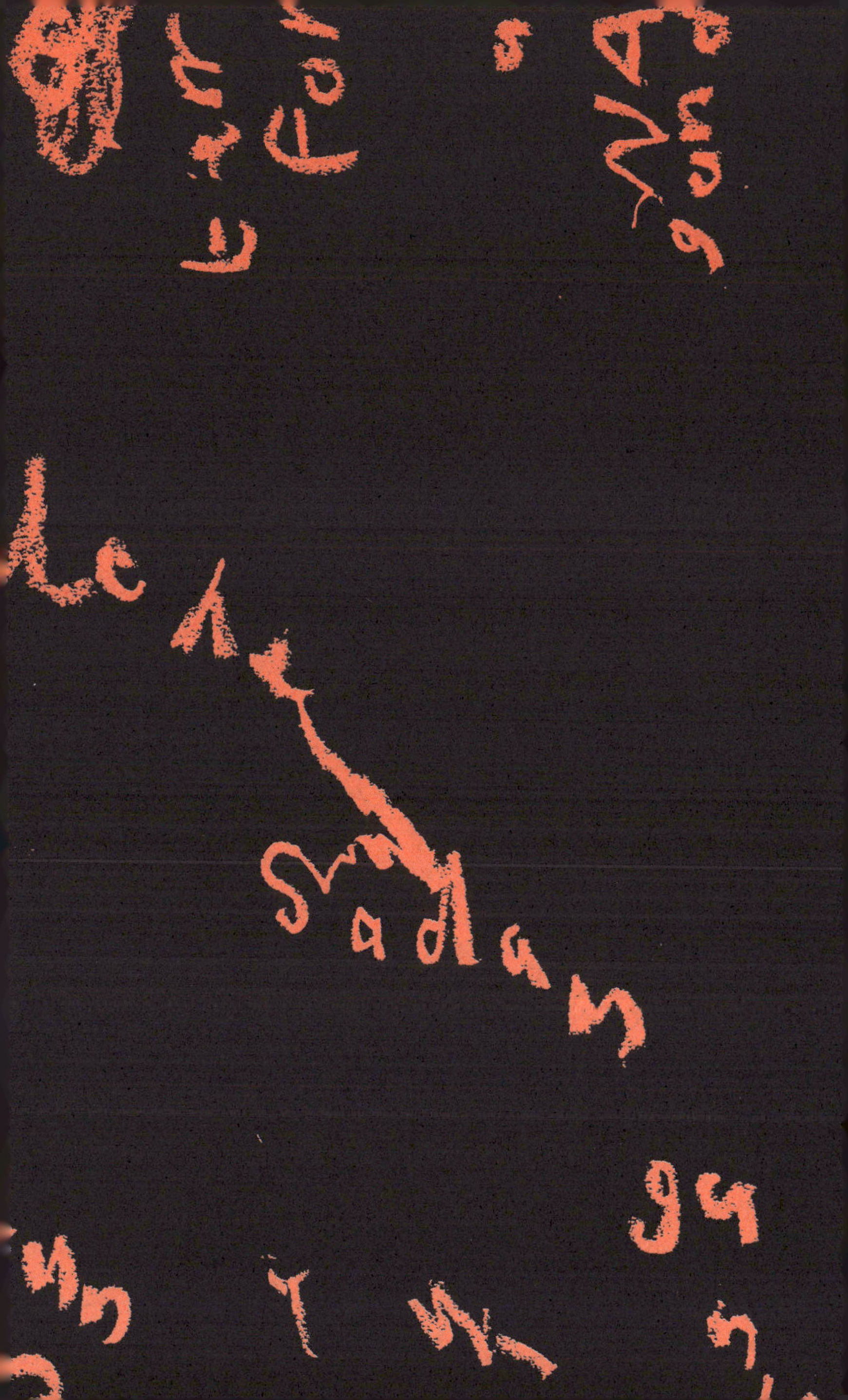
Sadang
94

Passages
Paysages
Passengers

i am gifted two pairs of gloves. because i live in Los Angeles, these feel like objects, props.

today is my birthday. my card is the Wheel of Fortune. it asks *What is the hand that turns the wheel*? K-Sue draws me the characters for the shaman ritual of riding the knives. in my automatic writing i ask—eyes closed, tongue prone, other handed:

Q: how do i ride?

A: *NA NUN DULCHE SADAM GANDA*

(Nayop calls as i'm writing and i ask her to translate: *I am the second person going)*

a candle burning on the altar explodes its glass when she speaks and i walk right into a fluorescent bulb. everything pierced, sharp dust.

i return to Cathy Park Hong's chapter in *Minor Feelings* on Theresa Hak Kyung Cha. a series of dreams and numbers leads Cha's brother to the site of her rape and murder. he finds her gloves: *They looked alive... They were her final art piece.*

Kathy invites me to reflect on Cha for a project at The Kitchen. i dig out my stack of Asian feminist zines traded for stamps in the '90s. i am 18 when i first see a photocopy of Cha's electric utterance, shattered sentences. i walk four miles to the used bookstore and buy *Dictee.* it is full of holes to breathe through. she cut the world i walk off.

i'm working on something else, but i keep returning to Cha. i do this for decades. in Cha's archives i notice a contact sheet of hands. the pictures are from 1982 and remain unfinished like her final film and book, *White Dust from Mongolia*. in the treatment for *White Dust*, she writes:

There exists a "Hole" in Time, a break in the linearity of Time and Space, and that empty space, the Absence, becomes the fixation, the marking that is the object of retrieval, a constant point of reference, identification, naming, the point of convergence for the narratives, the point of rupture, which gives, considers the multiplicity of narrative, multiplicity of chronology...

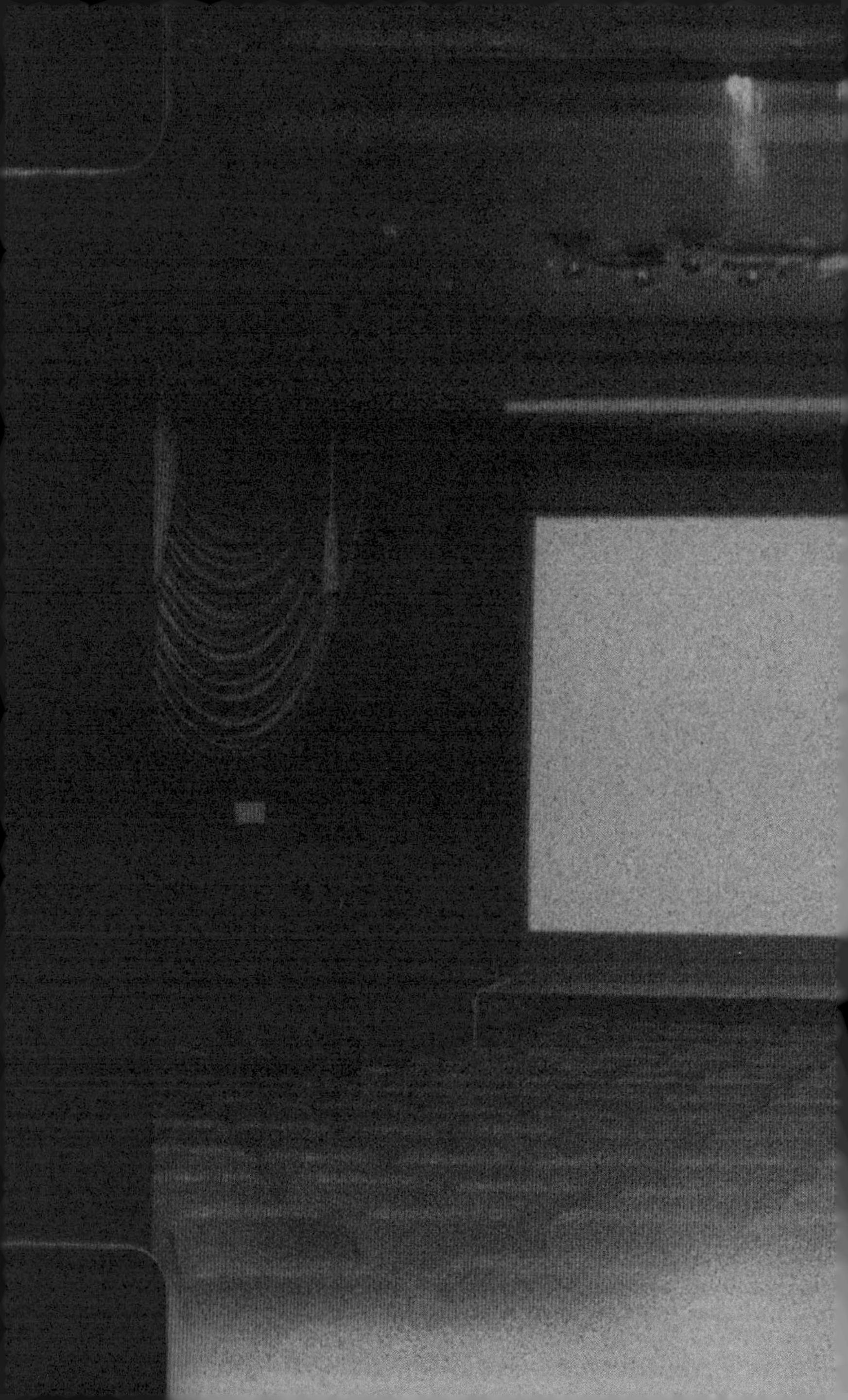

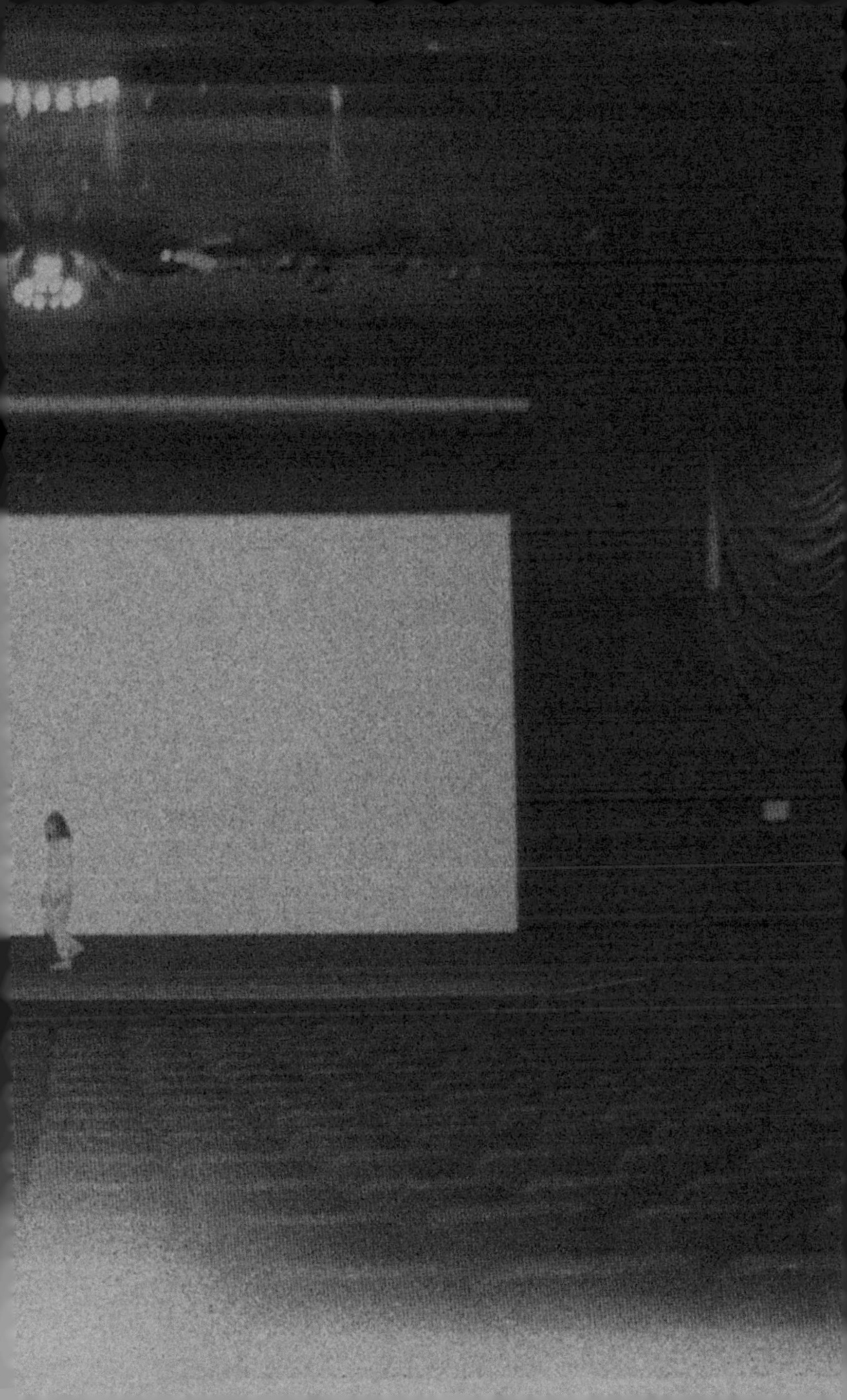

Cha describes two narrators: one in the past who is trying to remember and a second in the present who is trying to remember. throughout the piece the two points move toward each other to eventually form one complete *superimposition:*

It is Character #2 who returns, gives memory to Character #1. #2 is the retriever (the activator) of the memory of the narrative by the process of recounting the Récit...

#2 is one who searches #1.

my exhibition *contrapunctual* is postponed in March 2020. it's still simmering. the *contrapunctual* in the title comes from my automatic writing, not quite contrapuntal—a song with two different melodies playing simultaneously. i think of the word like a quantum superposition, the excess letters surface the puncture, punctum, in entanglement's time   science friction. Cha's description feels so familiar to my project. i consider filming the final scene of *White Dust*: Character #2 walks into a projection of train tracks.

Q: what if i record Cha's final scene?

A: *TESSERACT*
(a four-dimensional cube {4}x{4}, popularly used in science fiction to describe a portal to another world)

Brooke Intrachat is the other half-Asian girl from my hometown. in 2019 i run into her while working on *contrapunctual*. she is in Feng Shui school and offers to make a reading of the gallery. a Feng Shui reading produces an I Ching hexagram. for the postponed show, the hexagram is *44: 姤 (gòu) Coming to meet.* wind ☴ beneath heaven ☰, one punctured yin line beneath five solid yang lines. the Wilhelm/Baynes translation of *The Book of Changes* interprets: *The maiden is strong. Do not marry the maiden.* i interpret: *I may destroy you.* sensing for what is next in the work, i follow forty-four as it weaves in and out of these months.

there are forty-four days between Cha's death and my birth. a soul travels forty-nine days through the bardo. maybe we meet there? i look up shot forty-four in the *White Dust* storyboard. it is the same train tracks from the final scene, except Character #1 is inside the image, waiting.

Q: how do the two selves meet?

A: *SAMSARA SULLIGANG*
(cycle of life, death, rebirth. 강강술래 moon dance ritual. i decide to film a test tomorrow, the full moon.)

i pour water for the ancestors and Cha. i ask for her permission and their protection.

months ago my ancestors show me a tube, one in their hand and another like a channel of air. then i learn a Korean cosmology in which the first vibrations of the world emanate from flutes of air. so i tape a latex tube to a small microphone. it is sensitive to the touch but tonight it won't pick up my voice even with the amp turned high. i leave it on and begin recording the performance.

i use my infrared camera, which has been glitching ever since i take it to Korea to learn about shamanism. it repeats scenes from the past over the present, collapsing space-time like *Musok*.

i project Cha's train tracks, put on my gloves, and read out the automatic writing that led me here. an hour later i adjust the volume on the tube and suddenly so many sounds come out. new voices constantly clipped, broken. sometimes the whole phrase from a song, bells. it's like a radio, but i have no radio.

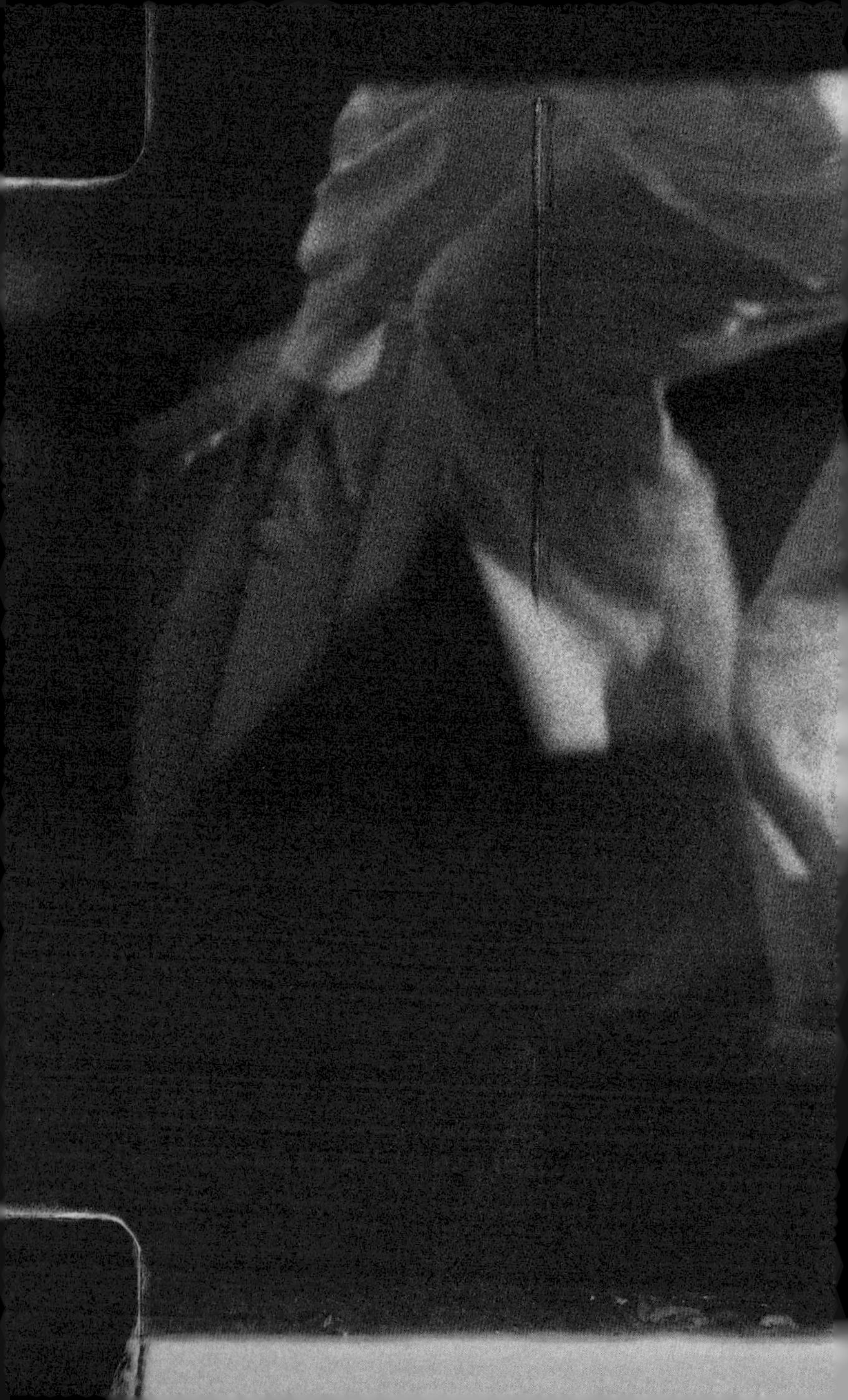

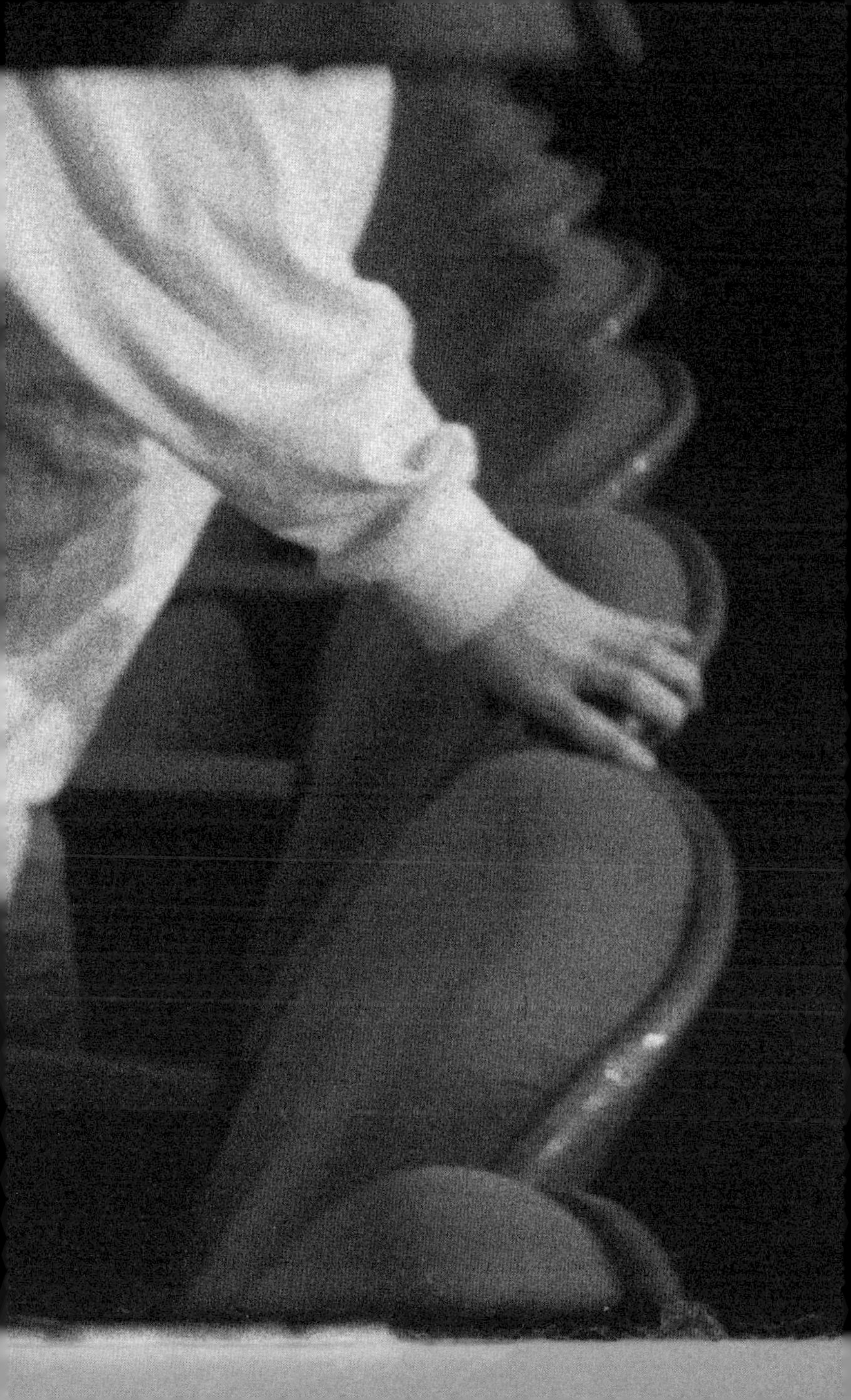

the footage comes out upside down and backwards, spreading horizontally like film, repeated in four frames.

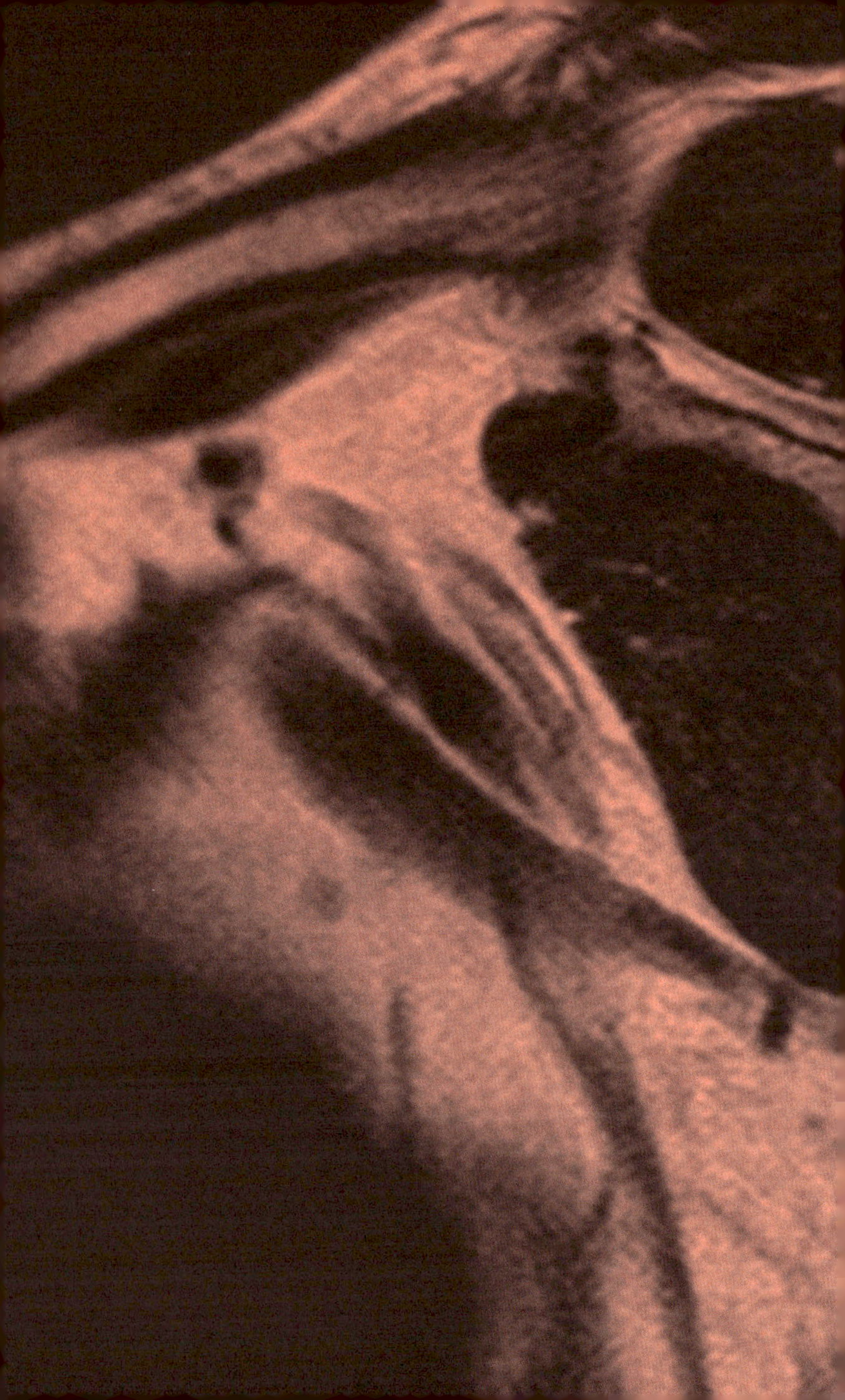

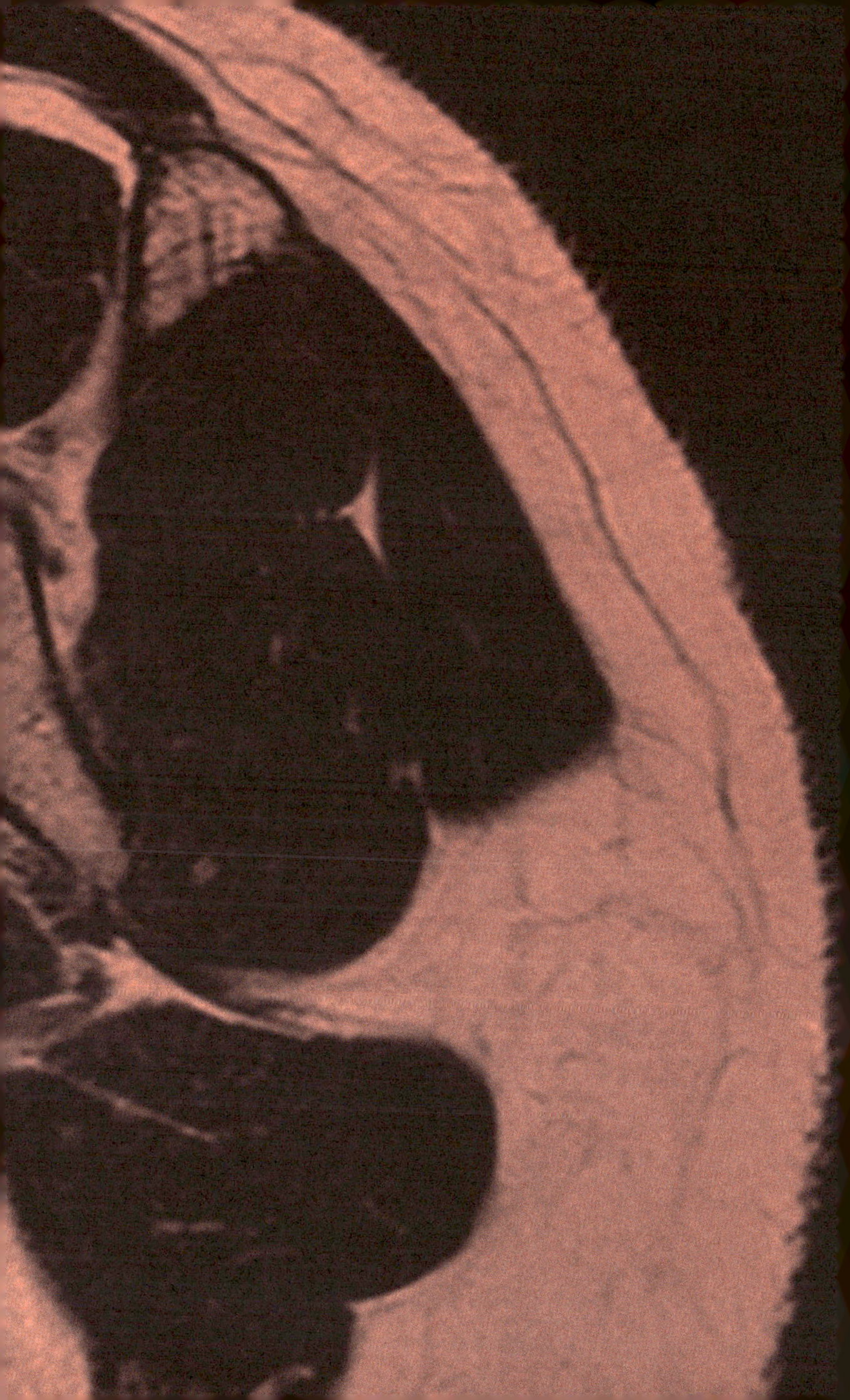

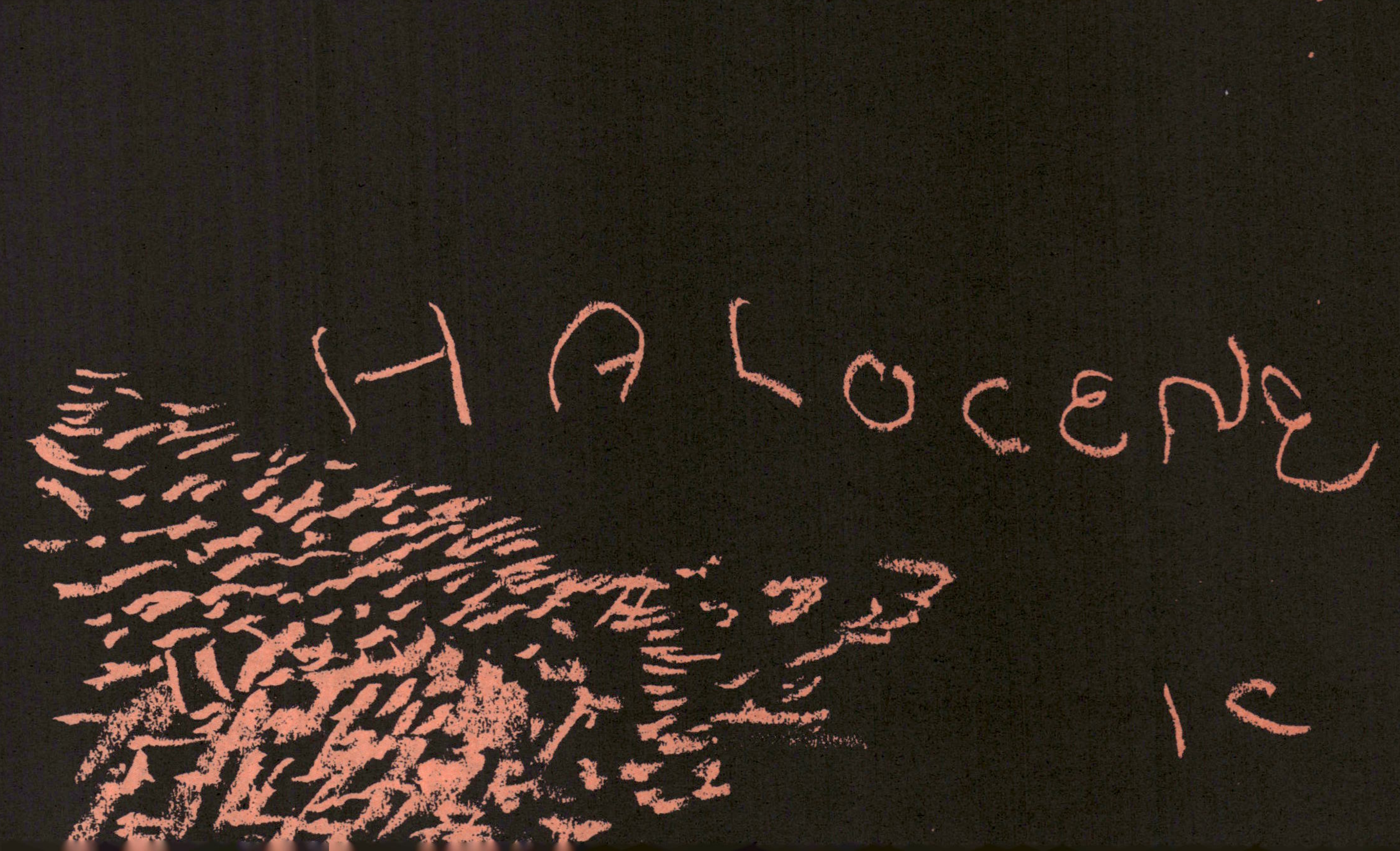
HALOCENE
1c

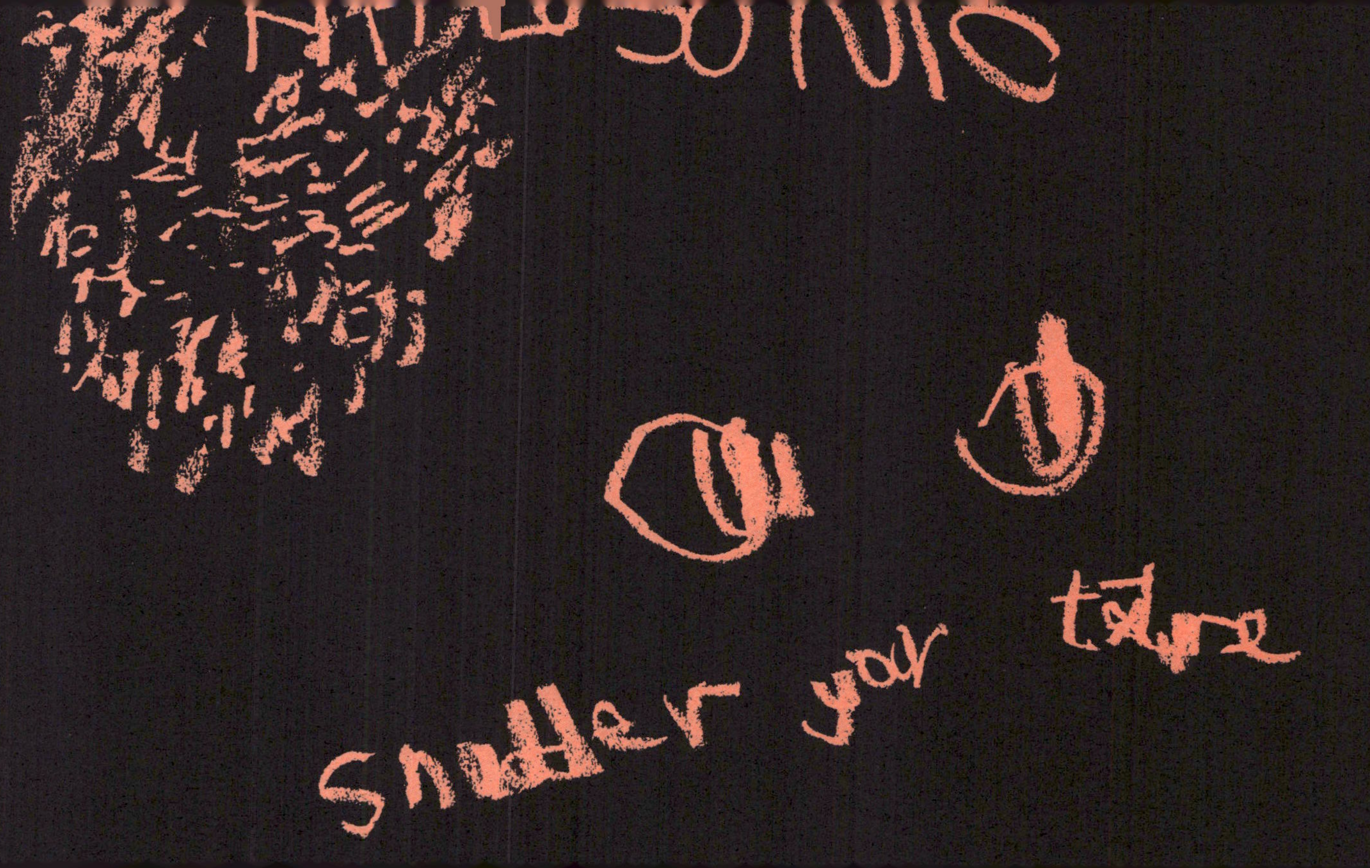
Shudder your

TIMESTAMPS, 3000 BC– 2022/06/05

1973/XX/XX

Perhaps the title of what I'm writing you should be something like this, phrased as a question: "What About Turtles?" You who read me would say, "It's true that it's been a long time since I thought about turtles."

—Clarice Lispector, *Água Viva*, 44.

3000~650 BC

a turtle crawls out of the Yellow River with the magic Lo Shu Square on its back. the arrangement informs the eight trigrams of the Bagua, Feng Shui, and the sixty-four hexagrams of the I Ching. Carl Jung coins the term "synchronicity" from his study of *The Book of Changes*. often conflated with chance, it refers to events that sync to a larger cycle, like the sixty-four codons of DNA, the sixty-four ancestors in seven generations, the sixty-four squares of chess.
how i am undone by it and the history i undo with it is holographic.

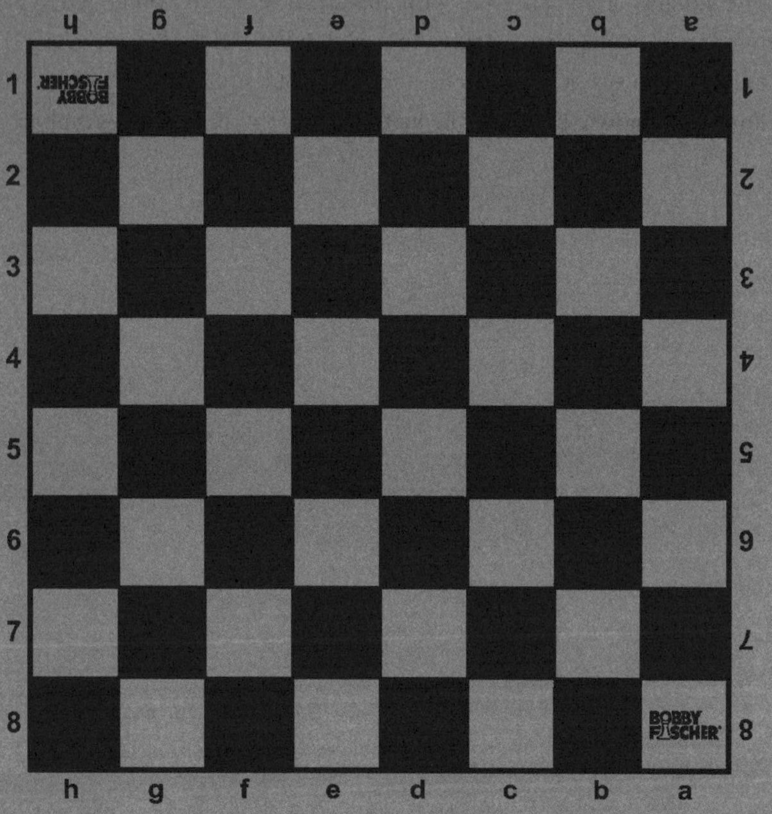

h g f e d c b a
1 2 3 4 5 6 7 8
BOBBY FISCHER
BOBBY FISCHER

TRIGRAMS UPPER ▶ LOWER ▼	Ch'ien ☰	Chên ☳	K'an ☵	Kên ☶	K'un ☷	Sun ☴	Li ☲	Tui ☱
Ch'ien ☰	1	34	5	26	11	9	14	43
Chên ☳	25	51	3	27	24	42	21	17
K'an ☵	6	40	29	4	7	59	64	47
Kên ☶	33	62	39	52	15	53	56	31
K'un ☷	12	16	8	23	2	20	35	45
Sun ☴	44	32	48	18	46	57	50	28
Li ☲	13	55	63	22	36	37	30	49
Tui ☱	10	54	60	41	19	61	38	58

Key for Identifying the Hexagrams

1980/XX/XX

All the elements I have outlined are encompassed in the larger context of MEMORY which I would develop in this book as a collective source, as almost having physical and organic dimensions, where space and time superimpose within it. It represents a body of time, units in time inside the time mass that is eternal and immeasurable, within which our existence is marked like a wound.
—Theresa Hak Kyung Cha, on *White Dust from Mongolia*

2019/04/10
scientists looking for data in black holes take their first pic of the center of galaxy M87. The hot blur around its negative space prefers not to, comes out like an aura photograph: *Strangers do not stay strangers for very long to those with an orange aura.*

2020/12/29

(how to enter?) *NEITHER NOR* 사이의 *LTTER* [illegible]

2019/04/11

when i send the picture to Bobby they reply, *That's haunted, you can't bring it home*. so i ship the dragon-limbed chinoiserie chair to the studio where it becomes an art problem and i immediately come down with a fever. after being sick in bed for weeks i make an appointment with Laura. while reading my energy, she says in an alternate lifetime concurrent with this one i am part of a mystery school called the Rosicrucian Cross. she says she doesn't really like parallel worlds, but my guides want me to know. i think of Brooke Intrachat, the other half-Asian girl from Lawrence, Kansas. i move away when i am eleven and my best friend calls to say she has a new friend who is also half-Asian. there is not another Asian person in our entire school. like a thread of my life spinning off and continuing. i return the following summer and meet Brooke. she is elegant, somehow so formed that her presence unties me from myself. it is thrilling to consider that i am actually spun from her. that "i" is neither singular nor solid, but the cut opening an invisible field. when Nayop is pregnant with me she has a *taemong* dream about Brooke Shields and growing up it is always *Brooke Shields went to Princeton, Brooke Shields has big eyebrows*. as a small child she draws my brows on when we leave the house, two thick marks hovering like a spell. i tell Brooke that Nayop almost names me Brooke, too. Brooke's mom has my name. twenty-five years later in Los Angeles i leave Laura's and drive to the grocery store. Brooke is standing in line at the counter. i ask if she remembers me. she says, *I've actually been thinking about you. Every time I go to San Francisco.* why are you going to San Francisco? *I'm studying Feng Shui at a mystery school.*

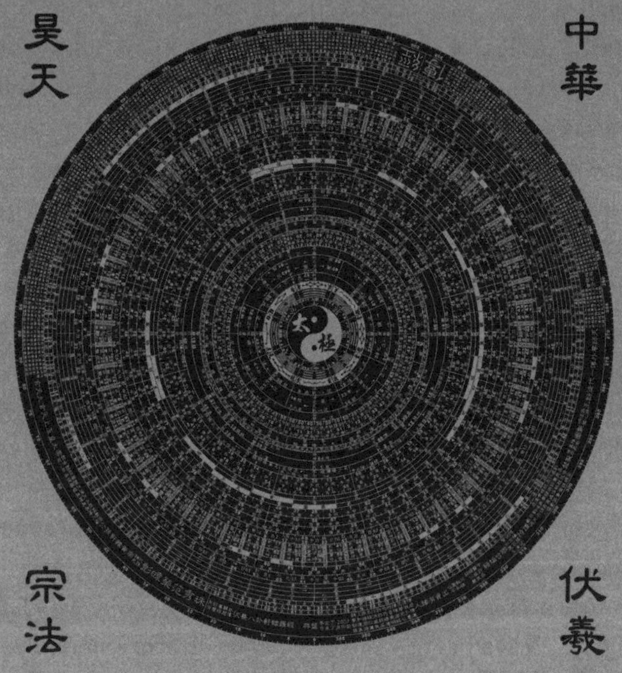
中華
伏羲
昊天
宗法

ephoto

PERMIS DE CONDUIRE

N° 1PMT 8L98 0617 1544 50US 05

Numéro ephoto

DÉMARCHE À SUIVRE :

1. Rendez-vous sur le site :
   https://permisdeconduire.ants.gouv.fr
   ou flashez le QR code ci-dessous
2. Remplissez le formulaire en ligne avec vos coordonnées personnelles
3. Dans le cadre identifiant ephoto, saisissez votre numéro d'identifiant ephoto inscrit ci-dessus
4. Attendez le traitement favorable de votre demande qui vous sera confirmé ultérieurement par courriel

Attention ! vous disposez de 6 mois à compter de la date de prise de vue pour effectuer vos démarches. Un délai d'environ 2H peut parfois s'appliquer entre la prise de vue et l'activation du numéro ephoto.

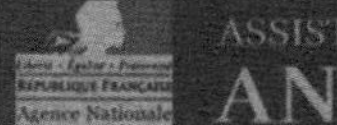

ASSISTANCE ANTS | https://permisdeconduire.ants.gouv.fr

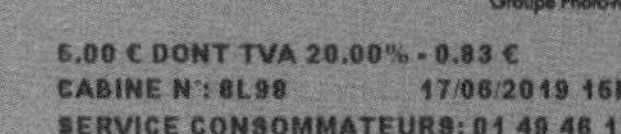

5.00 € DONT TVA 20.00% - 0.83 €
CABINE N°: 8L98 17/06/2019 16h45
SERVICE CONSOMMATEURS: 01 49 46 17 96

Votre signature

206 BC

the first compass, the Luo Pan, is created for Feng Shui, with an arrow magnetically aligned to the south. originally, only shamans use it to determine the site of burial for the dead. two red threads cross each other in the center. the face is called a rose.

2019/07/31
hi Brooke,
i keep imagining Feng Shui-ing a memory palace, like rearranging a room or the objects in a room of one's memory…i wonder if you might be interested in working with me on something? there is a piece of furniture i'm trying to understand.

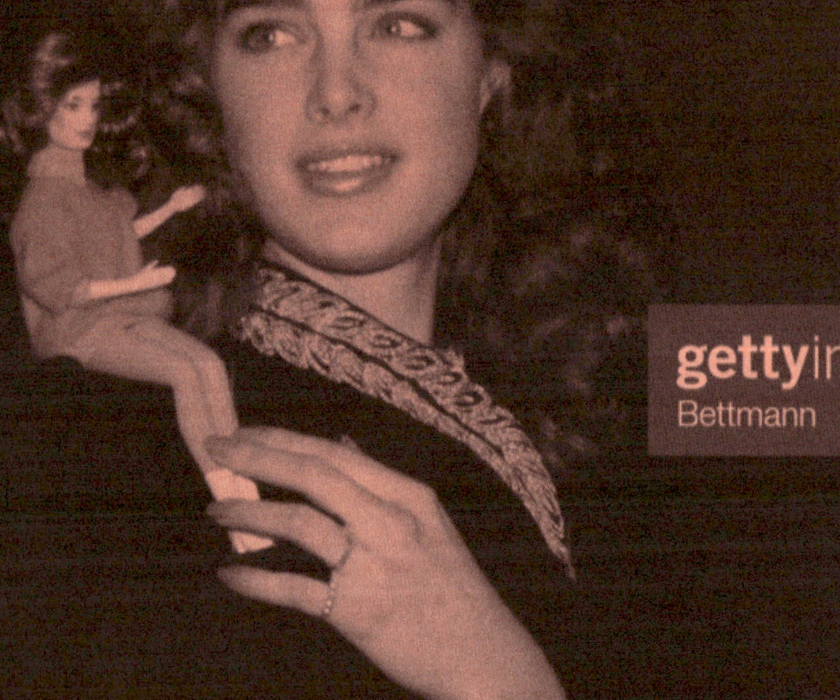

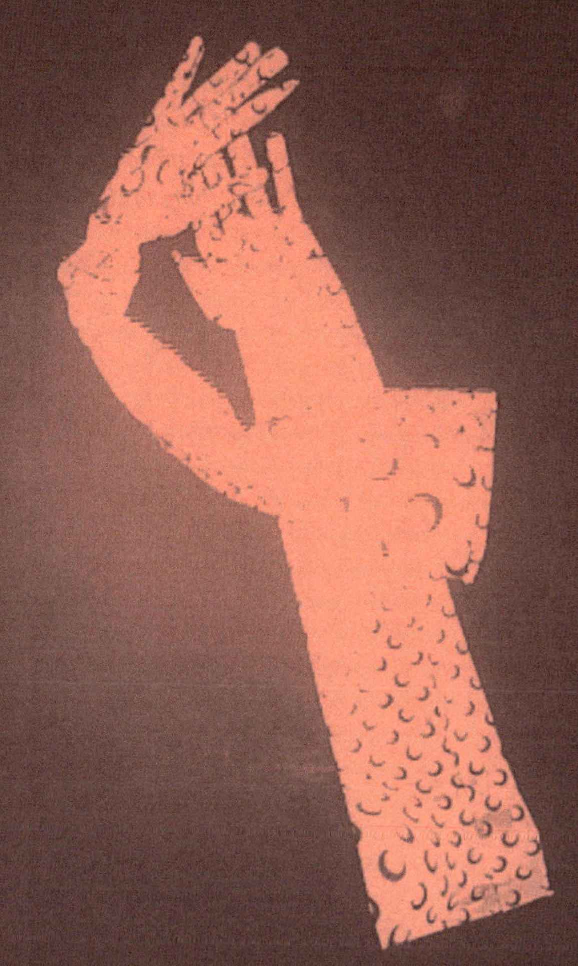

2019/08/01

The Chinese refer to the Bagua (the 8 symbols from the I Ching representing "principles" of reality and used in Feng Shui for placement) used for the living as the "Later Heaven" sequence or "manifested" sequence and the Bagua used for Feng Shui for the dead and their placement as the "Early Heaven" sequence or "before creation." I wonder which sequence would be used for this memory rearrangement? Something to think on.

—Brooke

2020/09/20

each of us is told to ask a question during the lecture about ancient Korean whale worship. i ask why the whale is never represented and depicted instead as a dragon. Helen says this is the wrong question. later that week in a meditation i'm asked, *How does it feel in your body?* and i realize i'm the only person sitting in water. i go to the emergency room. they find my shoulder is broken since the spring. they tell me to put all my weight on it and hold my breath for an hour. after emerging from the MRI i silently roll over and scream for a long time, reborn as pure sensation. the security guards keep saying, *But the test is over!* for months i cannot stop screaming. science has ten ways to describe pain. they are all numbers.

2008/07/11

i open page 44 of various books, looking for signs. *Dictee* has a photograph of Cha's mother. *The Poetics of Relation* is blank, opaque. in *Regarding the Pain of Others* there is a bus ticket to my parents' dating from 2008 when i return for the first time since being a teenager. in the hospital waiting room his colleagues, other white East Asian Studies professors, tell me in 1974 he says he is *Going to Korea to find a nice wife and then he sure did return with your mother! I remember her at a party in the very beginning but then she never really came around again.* the head of Korean Studies says *Korean women are crazy*. Nayop makes them uncomfortable. she is only friends with women who live outside. she is the best-dressed person in these rooms she does not care to enter. in the massive skater pants my brother and i abandon in the '90s, heels because the floors are all poisoned, a black vinyl trash bag under the bra drying from her neck, and Comme des Garçons cardigans she cuts the hearts out of. she is famous in all the rooms she does enter. one employee gathers all the other employees from the back of the grocery store to look at me, smiling, *You're that lady's daughter.* once she shoots a man with a bow and arrow in our house when it is time for him to leave. she receives a sign in a dream to buy the glass house on government auction after it is abandoned by the mob. on the floors in Atlantic City when she breaks even i say let's cash out and spinning the wheel Nayop says, *That's not how you play.* when i get into college, Nayop asks, *Princeton, like Brooke Shields?* and when i say no she asks, *Why don't you become an artist then?* i'm not an artist. i thought you wanted me to get good grades? i have better grades than Brooke Shields. *You must pass their tests because their tests are stupid. But don't believe in their world*. he wakes up from the coma and lives for eight more years.

2021/09/24

on a list of Korean names i notice Kwon means "tube." On a list of goddesses i notice Kwonyin is "She Who Perceives the Sounds of the World." in Yunuen's constellation before the last exhibition we ask the goddess Kwonyin to be our guide. she rides a dragon and dragon is my role. after a while, i understand my whole body is a throat. when i find the metal on the mountain its coil is long and shedding like snakeskin, so i take it home. the latex tube is used to pump mugwort through a fountain for three years, lucid stain spreading so it's seasoned. the I Ching says this will not end as it begins but in *harmony.* Best Buy has one microphone in stock. it is the circumference of the tube, made by Olympus, home of the gods. next to a diagram of a throat in *Dictee*, Cha says:

One by one. The Sounds. The sounds that move at a time.
stops. Starts again. Exceptions.
Stop. Start. Starts.
Contractions. Noise. Semblance of Noise.
Broken speech. One to one. At a time.
Swallows. Inhale. Stutter. Starts.

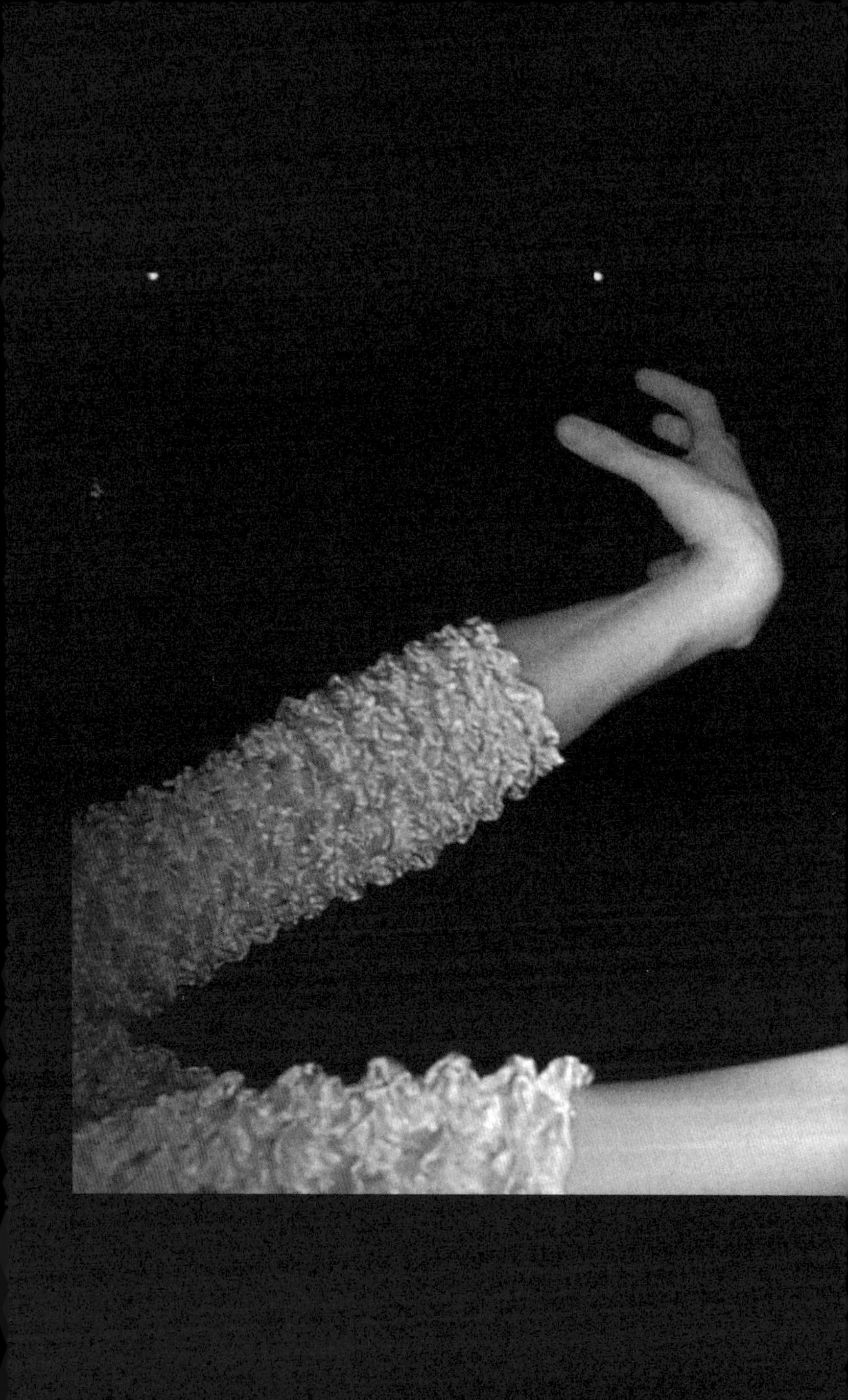

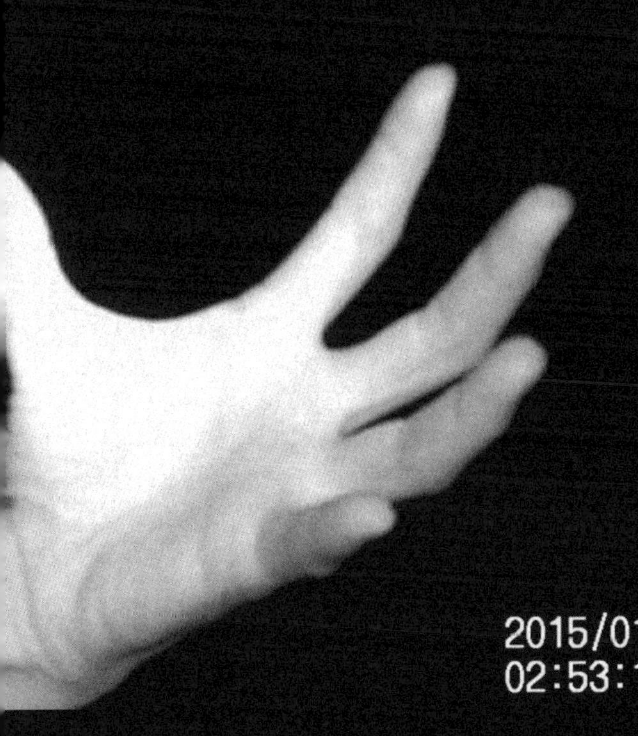
2015/01/22
02:53:10

2020/06/26

Chi Young asks me to picture the land of my mother's mother's ancestors. i remember my grandparents' paper house off a dirt road at the end of a long train ride south to the coast of Korea, the ocean, a beach. *Now walk until you see someone.* this seems impossible but she says *I will wait*, so i do, too. after a long time my grandmother appears. *Work only with ancestors well enough to heal the lineage, if they are not well, go back until you find someone who is.*
my grandmother is silent. her eyes are burned black holes. she is flat. she is paper. i'm scared i will not meet anyone else because i have no idea how i meet her but it doesn't feel right. i keep walking and see a bright light on the ocean. a beautiful woman wearing a massive metallic *hanbok* and jewels in her hair on a platform of lights waves slowly and i move onto the water toward her. she can't turn her body. she continues looking and waving at the beach. i begin to see her texture, graininess, and lines. she is video. i move further out onto the water. a third person appears. barely a teenager, she wears pants and where a face would be there is an opening to clouds. she stands on a raft holding a tall reed of bamboo. it is not for walking; it is not for paddling. it is hollow, a tube. and she is flesh. *Ask this lineage what they are known for.* she makes a channel of air inside the water, curling and extending it in every direction. it is a perfect negative of the tube in her hand.

2014/10/01

after the computer crashes, the whistling sounds of Haenyeo when they come up from diving is scattered all over my video. *A Woman Is Not a Woman* is made this way, beginning with a decapitated mermaid, in breaking waves, intangible heritage of held breath, breathing as dispersion. *Or it can crash.* here Nayop's own voice becomes permanently dubbed over by the Spanish-language translation of the only Korean soap opera on television. *Ellas me advirtieron que no debería ser tu amiga.* the oldest published mermaid sighting is written by the first European in Korea. i record Cha's words: *After having been, before having been.*

2020/12/27

(how do the two selves meet?) *TALL SAMSARA*

2020/08/11

i begin reading the Budoji, a prehistoric feminist cosmology of East Asia that was recovered in the 1980s. the opening lines tell of four heavenly beings building and tuning tubes that emit the first sonic vibrations in the universe. Helen says she translates it into English as *flutes* but sometimes they are made completely of air, so she starts calling them *tubes*.

2021/03/02

i looked up where the Budoji was discovered, thinking anthro dig in a cave, but the short Wiki says it was written and passed down through the Park family line (which we share, Nayop's maiden name) since Silla, until the only copy was lost while fleeing North Korea and then rewritten from memory. feels appropriate.

2021/03/02
So appropriate
It passed from paper to the body and then back again
I just read the chapter on Theresa Hak Kyung Cha and I'm crying
—K-Sue

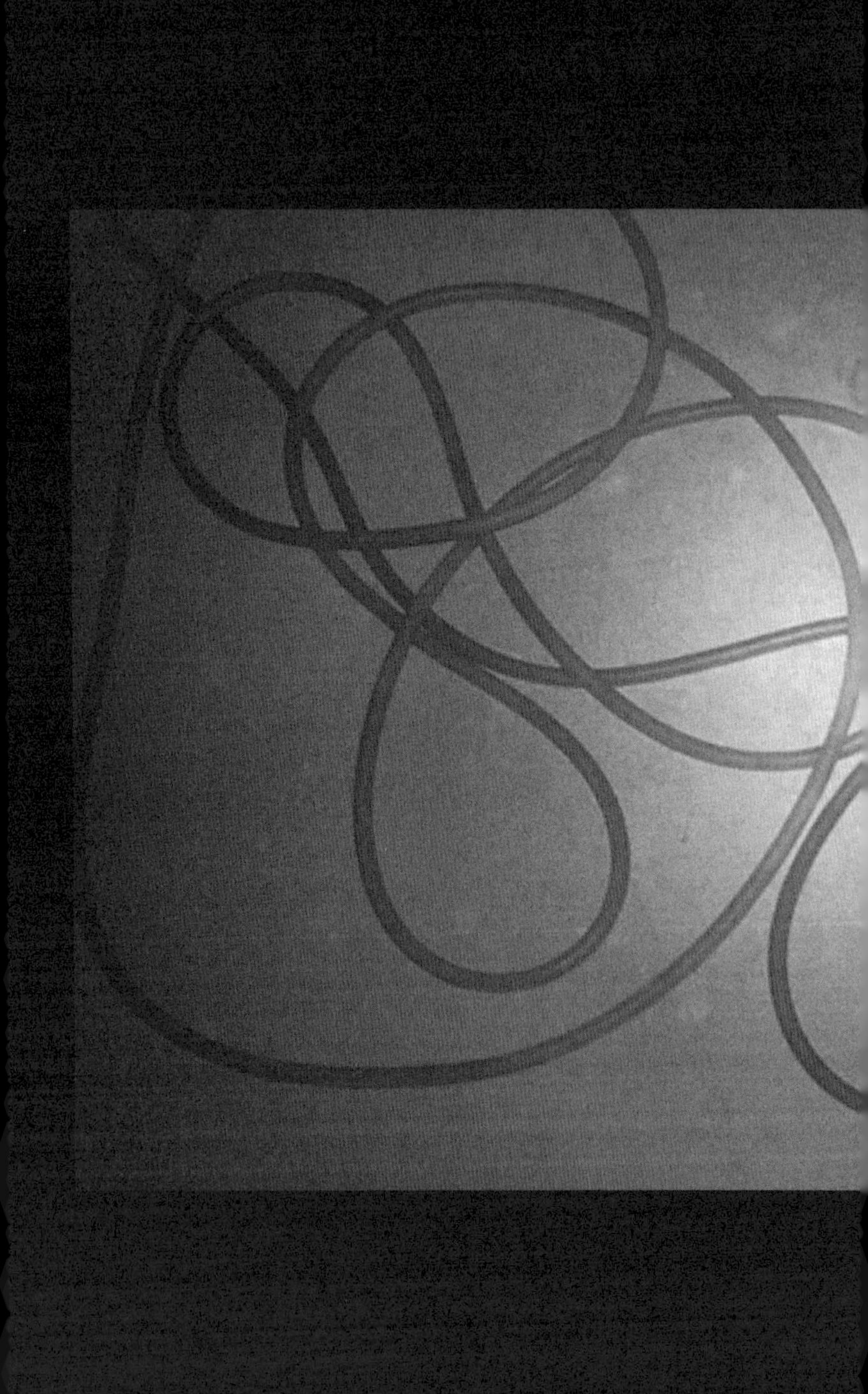

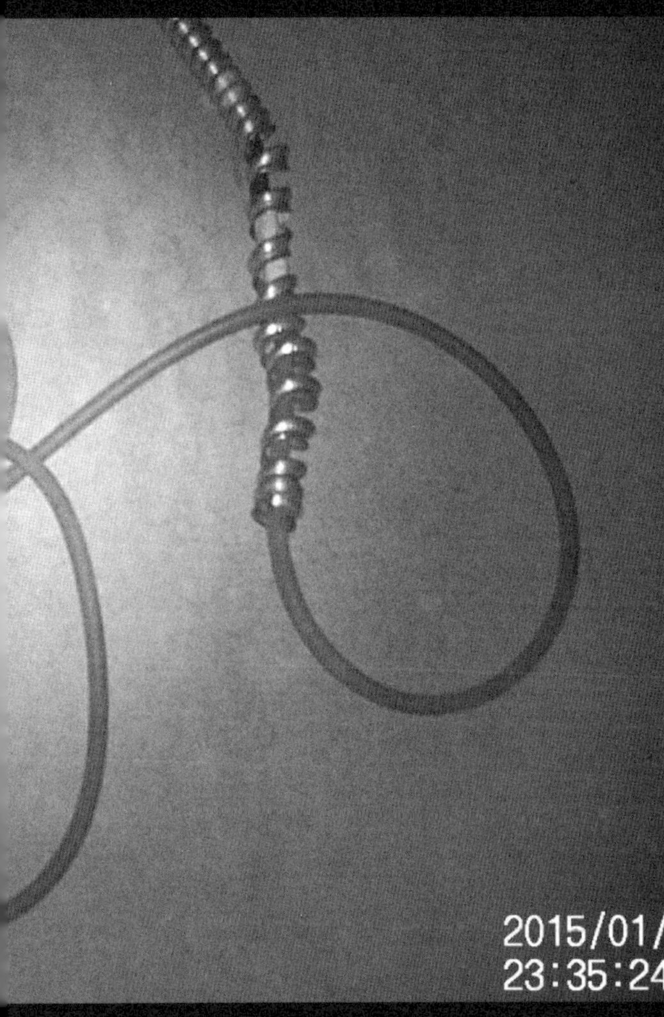
2015/01/10
23:35:24

2017/11/04

It's the story of everyone, even though that might seem weird and appropriative, but it's pouring out of a hole in outer space. i have no money and don't win any of the grants to go to Korea to learn about my family's shaman lineage, but Aja insists i'm supposed to go anyway. Saewon says, *Why don't we just go together?* a nuclear war seems imminent, so roundtrip tickets are only four hundred dollars. a pink credit card covered in holograms arrives in the mail.

2018/01/15
Saewon and i are invited to be in a show about witchcraft at a nuclear missile base. when i say there is a giant Korean bell on the land, noise blasts from the speakers in Saewon's living room. we yell to each other over the sound, jumping to turn them off. but they are not plugged into anything. we visit the bell. Sara comes with us and does an I Ching reading. we try to figure out how to ring the bell that is surrounded by ropes and tourists. eventually we crawl inside it and sing. we call the audio piece *Speaker Is a Microphone*. it begins and ends with Cha: *Tell me the story of all these things beginning wherever you wish. Let the sound enter from without.* the day after the opening, the installation we make inside of a gutted phone booth disappears and the Seoul Museum of Art invites me to a residency that starts immediately. i already have a ticket.

2017/11/01

i read the poet Kim Hyesoon's version of the myth, *Princess Abandoned*. Paridegi, the seventh daughter, is abandoned by the king and queen, then years later is asked to retrieve a flower and the Elixir of Life from the underworld to save them. filial exegesis misses her desire. she goes towards the dark. Paridegi is rewarded with a place to live in the kingdom, but she chooses to heal the dead. moving between worlds, she becomes the first shaman. *Paridegi's father came to know he was dead through death. At that instance, the medicinal water Paridegi brought him, the poison, the gift of that realization, is what saved him inside death. Lao-tzu referred to this state of being alive inside the space of death as nothingness* mu *and called it* hyônbin 현빈. Hyôn *is something closed, something black. And* -bin *signifies a woman's reproductive organs, the mouth of a metal lock, a valley. The place that Paridegi goes to, travelling through death, is an empty place because it is a feminine space.*

202X/03/17

i paint my teeth black. and if i smile, it is the abyss. and if he lives, he lives in my house.

2021/03/18

(how to rise?) *TERRANTULA CELLAR SHRED* (what is in the cellar?) *STIGMA*

1915/XX/XX

great grandmother, mother of Pae Il Op, born in the South Jeolla province. she is a widow. villagers come to her when they are sick. she tends a tree with white fabric.

1991/05/XX

Changok is the youngest of Nayop's siblings. he teaches me to draw a rose, a tree, arms undone. my foot is caught in his motorcycle wheel. he crashes his motorcycle crossing into North Korea and loses his face. when he returns no one recognizes him and no one speaks to him.

2018/01/20

i read reports that tigers—a shaman spirit god and symbol of Korea hunted to extinction by the Japanese military—have been spotted in and around the DMZ. witnesses say the tigers sound like *motorcycles revving.*

1935/XX/XX

Schrödinger's cat is a thought experiment that illustrates a paradox of quantum superposition. In the thought experiment, a hypothetical cat may be considered simultaneously both alive and dead as a result of its fate being linked to a random subatomic event that may or may not occur.

2018/08/08

i call Brenda, the animal psychic in Florida with the landline, and ask if she can help me find the tigers. Brenda says the tigers are not afraid, *Their freedom comes from within. They don't want to be found but they want to talk.*

2019/11/01

the person sitting next to me on the plane apologizes for smelling like smoke, *It's the wildfires in Malibu.* while in Portland, i learn Mikhail is the oldest living Korean tiger in captivity and lives in the zoo there. when i go to meet him, there is a sign that says *No animals currently on view.* he dies the day before.

2018/11/06

i read that A. Turiyasangitananda Coltrane’s Sai Anantam Ashram in the Santa Monica mountains has been burned in the fires. several articles say it is destroyed but one mentions that the stairway remains.

2015/02/25

i visit Inwangsan, a mountain in Seoul where shamans live in tents. flames encased in glass, offerings of peanut chips and soju. i do not film them, i follow their cats. we move far from everyone to a flat dirt landing and in the center, in brightest red, a free-standing staircase.

2016/02/10

she asks me what i see and i see nothing. i mean, i see her. i mean, it hasn't started yet. i'm not in a trance. she says, *This is it, this is all of it. Just tell me the first thing that comes to your mind.* the shame we are given is the only door to cross, the hardest door. finally, i tell her about the necklace in the sky. that it is anime. i see Inwangsan and cry at the immensity, say i am sorry i have only just seen you and the mountain says, *We do not need to be seen to exist.* many familiar images: Hiroko Tamano, the first female Butoh dancer whose class i take in Berkeley once, is preparing the floor, towel wrung like a monkey's tail. and the Sai Anantam Ashram where i visit once, which Turiya is asked by God to build in 1976.

2016/03/02

i write to Hiroko and she says i must come to Portland in a few weeks but i cannot afford to fly there. the next day David Duchovny is filming a detective show on my street and offers me six hundred dollars to use my driveway. *The truth is out there*. the Portland Institute of Contemporary Art asks if i want to do a performance. i'm already on the plane.

2016/03/06

i visit the Sai Anantam Ashram and meet Brahmashakti Fudail. she describes being a teacher on the East Coast decades ago and attending a talk by Turiya, then packing up and moving to Sai Anantam the next day. we talk about how the ashram is for sale and what could be done to stop it. i get a copy of Turiya's book, *Monument Eternal*. on the way home i have a reading with Marty. she says i am not to intervene in the ashram. there is something else to learn from it. i struggle with this but suddenly another coma comes and i must prepare for Na.

2019/04/22

the ashram is sold before the fire to developers who never develop anything, so no one is there when it happens. it is surrounded by a barbed wire fence now. i slip under and down the hill. everything is alive. the flowers and grass and animals are loud, grown back strong from ash. i walk across the rushing stream and a grey pelican, mouth full, sails down right above my head, holding the light like a breath: in ancient Egypt, the animal of safe passage through the underworld. i reach the massive swirling white steps ascending to the sun. a ruin ruining time's measure, a monument eternal. i cannot remember the small building that was here except that it had a blue carpet, the color of all this sky. for the first time my infrared camera records a glitch not in image but in sound.

2019/06/16

i call Grace and tell them i'm in Paris to see King Tut. he came to Los Angeles last time so it's my turn. they tell me to pay attention to everything that happens tomorrow. they say it may not come in complete sentences. they say to make an offering. they say Basquiat did his spell in the open. they say to pull books off a shelf and choose any line. they say to make my own deck of cards. they ask me what my clair is and i say clearly not claircognizance because i have no idea what i'm doing. i say except i know about next season's accessories, so maybe Claire's Boutique?

1965/XX/XX

You don't know what a female is, you desexed monstrosity.

—Valerie Solanas, *Up Your Ass*, quoted in Andrea Long Chu, *Females*, 44

2019/06/17

at 10:30 am the full moon is in my sun Sagittarius, making a direct line with the Earth and the massive black hole at the center of the Milky Way galaxy, Sagittarius A*. i am in a room of one hundred and fifty objects Tutankhamun uses to travel to the afterlife. from inside my sleeve i scatter the Emma Kunz crystal dust that i get in Switzerland days ago. her geometric drawings tell her how to heal people. they look like timelines. at her Grotto, the attendant says we cannot just walk to the very back, which is marked with a green crayon. it is too strong. we have to work our way up. i feel like using the dust, which is what the Grotto is made of, you are already green and everything leading up to green. i play Turiya's ashram tapes against the soundtrack pumped into the room. in the 1980s God asks her to sing, which is not a part of her music practice. she records the songs in private and when she plays them for the ashram members, someone says, *This man's voice is beautiful. Who is he?* in some versions of the myth, Paridegi must pass as a man to enter the underworld. Joan of Arc burns in soldier's armor. the press that follows Tut's new irradiated rendering is outraged by his *feminine hips, budding breasts, club foot.*

2019/08/05

Cryotypes may not be conventionally genetically related (in the "tree of life" sense) but they share a different kind of genetic relation—that of evolutionary physiology (the mode of life sense): the shared acquisition of a specific adaptive suite.

1968/XX/XX

King Tut's penis declared missing.

2019/06/17

i record Tut's golden nails and shoes in case he wants to follow me out of the looted headset polo porn park constructed around his passage, whispering apologies for our ugly world. walking through the doors i hear music outside. in front of the Grande Halle a group of Asian women dressed casually in different colors and prints are performing a synchronized dance. there is not one way to face it, like an impossible shape. the dance doesn't rest, it rotates. not for looking, beauty is suddenly the least we can do, the most we can do. at the center of the formation one dancer wears striped pants, a tiger on her shirt.

2014/08/26

Sanrio announces Hello Kitty is not actually a cat but a girl in the style of a cat.

2019/08/04

(what am i making?) *TELL NEW GENTLE RELATION VIEWS UPON ONTOLOGY CRYOTYPE* (and the tiger?) *TIE OFFERING UP SUBTERFUGE ELLE CLARION.*

2019/6/17

i arrive at the address in the Left Bank where the bookstore is and it is not here. instead there is a Claire's fucking Boutique. i have never seen one outside of a 1990s American mall. i search the store for a sign and everything is obstinate. i think maybe just hoops but there are hundreds of earrings and no hoops. it's almost like they don't sell jewelry, like how salad is always made of meat. in my final lap i see something. i place it on my head, is it a crown? walking outside, i start to see signs for the Pompidou and remember their bookstore.

2019/02/19

a pipe bursts in Nayop's house and the Fire Department reports her to the city for being a hazard. Na has three weeks to clear *all debris or be fined $2,000 a day.* Nayop and i are both engaged in research. a lot of her research is paper bags lined with paper bags, at the heart a towel folded down to its smallest cell, labeled with a date in marker and inside, a single hair or a gold cross. the house is striated beneath particles of dust uncanny in scale, a diorama of Pompeii made by a child from cotton balls: it's not length, it's speed, nothing, more. tossed clothes bully furniture crushing their knees, a vase of reeds face down in a cracked bath surrounded with trick mirrors. i am cleaning it for years already. i find several letters from my father about what a real Korean woman is like. i make a sparking joy box. each night we leave and stay at a hotel where Nayop won't watch the *Konmari* show. *My Cousin Vinnie* is on and after a while she yells, *Nothing in this movie is beautiful and people only arguing about words!* i find *Orlando* and immediately fall asleep. in the morning Nayop's face is right above mine: *I've been waiting for you to wake up to talk about the movie! It's about how to be an artist, how you have to live many lifetimes. You have to watch it to learn!* the hotel is a few blocks from Nayop's, except this part of the street has a different name. it's called the 38th parallel. there is a Korean War memorial here in downtown Philadelphia. each day we cross the 38th parallel and pass all the guys dressed as Benjamin Franklin to go home. one day there is a wreath that says *BEST FRIEND* hanging on Nayop's house. cops come later and tell us about a motorcycle accident. they ask why we're wearing hazmat suits. *The dust.* i find a tiny book inside Nayop's couch in the style of a Hindu prayer manual, a drawing of Hanuman on the back. Litia tells me the flying monkey god is cursed to forget his power but asked to jump to another country. i buy the book at the Pompidou when i am 18.

2001/03/20

last year i drop out of high school and this year i drop out of college after one in four or everyone i can remember is raped, and i listen to all the library's audio cassettes of *À la recherche du temps perdu* each night while sleeping in the bunkbed above my roommate and her boyfriend and his gun because *Remembrance of Things Past* is also translated as *In Search of Lost Time*, as if we can retrieve it from wherever it went, not here, a town where dancing is actually illegal, a small joke to my revolution, but maybe i'll find the time in France because it is far and i can stay at this lesbian tour guide's apartment. at Charles de Gaulle airport security detains me because they think i am a man with a bomb and the waiters at the restaurant next to the apartment mime sex and say *American!* my body is excessive. the song *She's Like the Wind* keeps playing in all the train stations. i sing it back in French, trying to immerse in something that's not here. it rains everyday so i mostly eat bread and watch videos on the Pompidou TVs and hang out in the bookstore. when i end up back at Nayop's she says, *I don't speak English I don't know what that means* and doesn't speak English to me for days until one day she says, *I've never felt like a real woman. I've never been in love.*

2019/06/17

a sweaty man rushes up to me *Chinoise?! Japonaise?! Coréene?!* over and over, breathless. *You marry?! You marry?! You marry?!* then he starts to make a crude motion with his hands, a wedding ring on and off. i walk over to a section of Basquiat's journals. an Asian woman hands me the display copy. i open to a page that says only *A crescent sun.* another book shows a drawing of Joan Jonas's dog with four eyes. a catalogue on the cosmos is propped open to images from *The Book of Fixed Stars*. i buy seven postcards and back at the apartment i cut them in half with a knife and without looking assign each piece something that i am following, something that is following me.

2001/04/10

back at the anarchist bookstore i work at in high school as if i never left except now i don't believe in do-it-yourself, in "your" or "self." in this bare field the small zine *external text* written by Yumi Lee, a teenager from Kansas, arrives with a photocopied image from Theresa Hak Kyung Cha's *Dictee* on the cover. she breaks language and language is law. i go out and find the book, used, half-off, covered in tombs, death stuttering, spitting, repeating, jagged lineage of martyrs, origin hissing an electromagnetic line not visible, not redaction, empty pages ring at decibel of void, some parts of the text are nothing more than raised flesh, *texere.* refusal plays its puncture, the held breath balloons into consciousness, into another animal's verb, talisman not given but going. i do not understand her as intimately as i do not understand myself.

2022/06/05

in the elevator to the *Dictee* reading a writer tells me the memoir is about her Korean mother's schizophrenia. pressure chambers open the Eustachian tubes, the Middle Ear. Pop. *Are you biracial? The number of Asian women who become schizophrenic after marrying white men is extremely high.* i point out there is no button for the fourth floor.

2001/09/11

during Eye Movement Desensitization and Reprocessing the therapist gets up and says, *We must evacuate the building.* she leaves the room before me and as i pass the desk i see her notebook, a page that says only *Asian mother, weak.*

2021/10/12

Nayop wants to call at 4 but waits until 5 because it's bad luck. tetraphobia is because "four" sounds like death in Korean and other Asian languages, 사 *sa*. in buildings the fourth floor is often unmarked, a void. Nayop is calling to say my real art is to invent a new color. she's been saying this for years. this time she says, *It's something like pink*. i start to see it with my eyes closed, an afterimage. after green. next to red.

2019/06/17

at one of the photobooths all over the Paris subways i take a driver's license picture. the machine has many government regulations on the final image and rejects all of my attempts until accepting one, just the crown of my head.

2019/07/12

i keep repeating *a crescent sun with double eyes*, until the warm net lights up over me: it's an eclipse. i return to the ashram with an offering as moon takes sun. the hills are bleached blonde now and i move into the trees. a single laminated piece of paper from Sai Anantam remains affixed to one and i read aloud: *Going in, I bring my attention to the omnipresent truth of God. At this very moment, I open up my being.*

the stairs glitch.

2018/04/25

the very important scholar asks if my great grandmother is a famous shaman. *Musok* is outlawed during the Japanese Occupation and Korean women with children are referred to by their child's name so no one in my family can even remember what she calls herself.

2019/08/26

Turiya chooses her name, which means “the fourth”: supreme consciousness after conscious, subconscious, unconscious. at her party they tell a story about how Turiya was seated on an airplane next to Mother Theresa and after talking a while they learn they]are born the same day.

2018/04/19

i move back to Seoul during the season of Yellow Dust. on Jeju Island my infrared camera begins to glitch, scenes from the past return in scenes of the present, bodies double, triple, traverse, borders collapse since the beginning, *born, spinning*. a timestamp shudders between 2017 and 2014 with seconds snapping to an invisible beat. the video changes with each viewing and when the glitch mutates into new form i know another chapter begins.

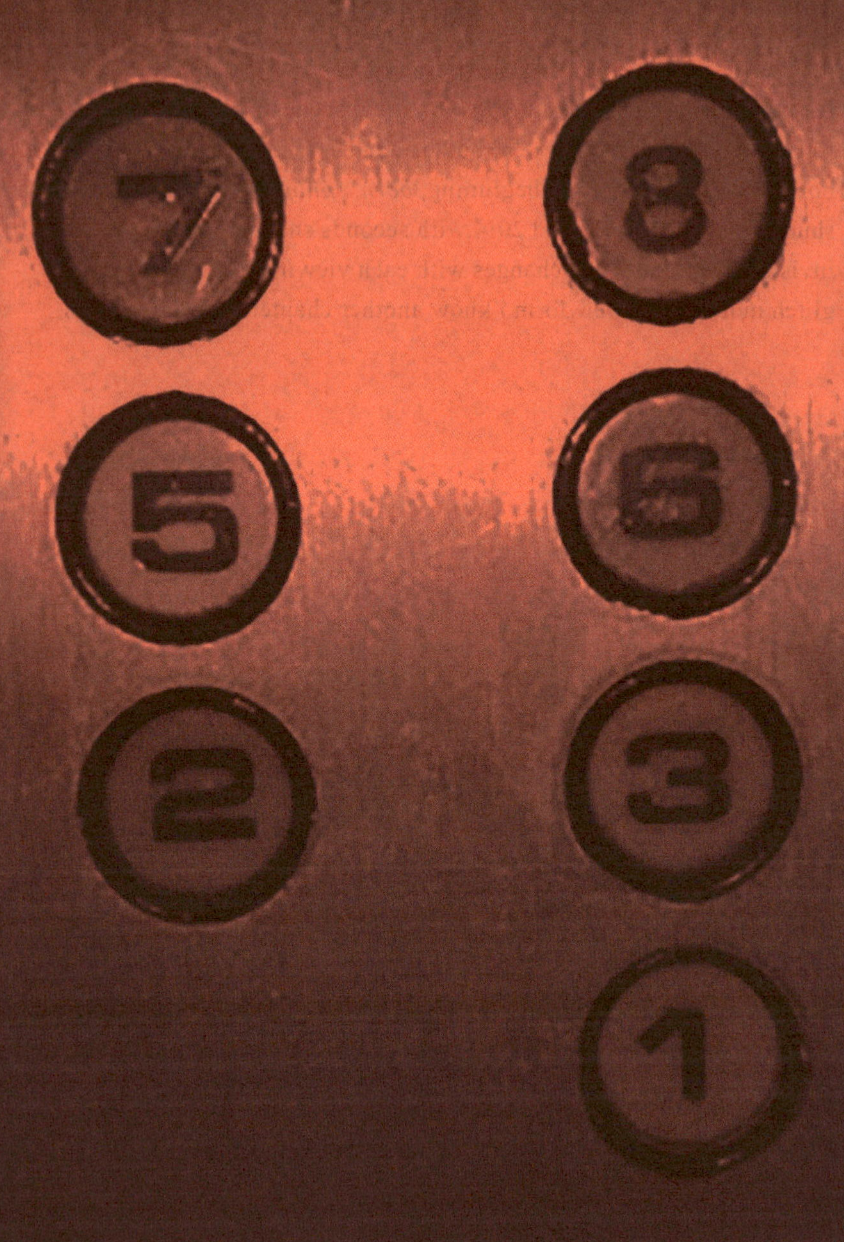
7
8
5
6
2
3
1

كوكبة الرامي على ما يرى في الكرة

القلادة

النعايم الواردة

النعايم الصادرة

وكواكبه ثلثون كوكبا

2018/04/25

the scholar asks if i have a business card. Saewon tells him she makes flower essences. he asks if we are making a documentary with HBO. then two people from HBO arrive. the HBO people ask what camera i'm using. i try to describe how it doesn't really have a viewfinder, it's supposed to be held by trees. his assistant gives a tour. Saewon and i ask, why the mostly female shamans work with only male gods? he pulls a heavy shroud off a canvas to show a painting of three women that is almost identical to the painting of three men next to it. he says some gods used to be female and then they were all changed to male. only on Jeju are the female gods still worshipped. *And snakes.* at the end we ask if he knows anything about Paridegi. he walks us over to a locked door and opens it to reveal a room with the only mannequin we've seen, dressed in many colors surrounded by props. he locks the door again and says, *But none of this is real.*

1993/XX/XX

the girl fits her body in
to the space between the bed
and the wall. she is a stalk,
exhausted. she will do some
thing with this. she will
surround these bones with flesh,
she will cultivate night vision.
she will train her tongue
to lie still in her mouth and listen.
the girl slips into sleep.
her dream is red and raging.
she will remember
to build something human with it.

—Lucille Clifton, “night vision,” in *The Book of Light*, 44

2018/04/27

the scholar invites us to a *gut*. there are lots of cameras and reporters in the small house. after some hours of ritual, the *Mudang* opens the floor for the audience to dance. i record this and a cameraman says, *You're wasting your time. Wait until later when she brings out a pig's head and swords. That's what everyone wants to see.* outside Saewon and i find a shack built with tarps and corrugated plastic around a tree. inside a painting of women around a tree covered in fabric, fire, and liquid offerings below. it's like the phone booth on the missile base where we put Saewon's flower essence and my raincoat. we ask the scholar what this place is, and he says it's not important, it's just an offering that has to be made to the land. as we leave, the scholar gives us each a box and inside is a commemorative towel from the shaman. every day since i arrive in Seoul i ask for and do not receive a towel. not from the gods, just from the residency manager. this towel is hot pink. nearby, Kim Jong-un crosses the border to the South.

2020/12/27

i start only asking with the non-dominant part of my body and humming, singing, screaming because this vibration changes the pain that spirals down my other arm. this hand is fluent in something unfamiliar to me. this hand only wants to write red. i ask questions and wait. listen for a sound that i sound out, follow my tongue rising, *ssssssss* utterance. i have to look up the words that arrive: *The fourth dimension of a cube, Portal, A Wrinkle in Time, Unfolds into a net of faces*, 누구에게 *TO WHOM*, because time can be repaired, is *born, spinning.*

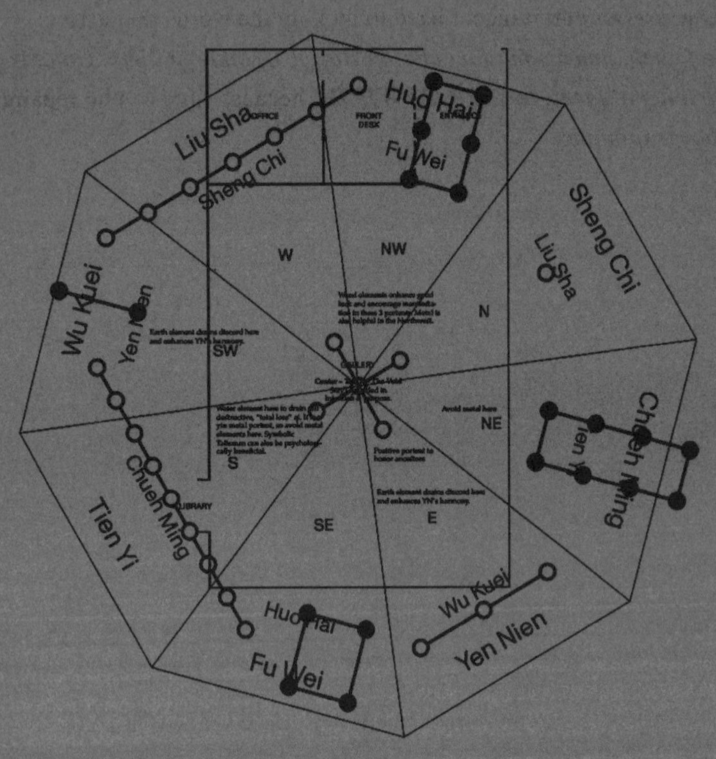

Liu Sha
OFFICE
FRONT DESK
Huo Hai
Fu Wei
Sheng Chi
W
NW
N
Sheng Chi
Liu Sha
Wu Kuei
Earth element drains discord here and enhances YN's harmony.
SW
Avoid metal here
NE
Positive portent to honor ancestors
S
Chueh Ming
Chuen Ming
LIBRARY
Earth element drains discord here and enhances YN's harmony.
SE
E
Tien Yi
Wu Kuei
Yen Nien
Fu Wei

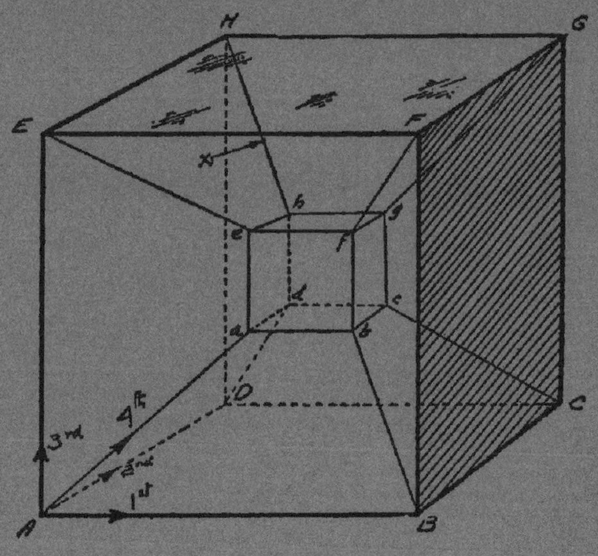

H
G
E
F
X
h
g
e
f
d
c
a
b
D
C
3rd
4th
2nd
1st
A
B

1914/XX/XX

Charles Hinton writes the first descriptions of the tesseract using colors that intersect along imagined planes: *We must not think of a four-dimensional body as formed by moving a three-dimensional body in any direction which we can see.* cube touching cube between time, at the edge of everything a beginning.

1980/XX/XX

Cha describes the end:

19. On the screen is projected same shot of railroad tracks

20. The woman enters live from screen left

21. She walks into the image slowly

The image behind dissolves from CLS to MS to LS

She physically enters the image

22. Fade to white

23. Image of the same room projected on the screen. The camera tracks back revealing the screen periphery. Revealing the room in which the image is projected

1898/XX/XX

Brooke sits with the chinoiserie chair. she says it needs to be burned. not up or down: black. i hate the chair but she is tender with it. *It's like us*. i only remember meeting my father's parents a few times. they don't approve the marriage, but they do collect Asian antiques. even Josie Packard is allowed to stay in *Twin Peaks* as furniture. so after they all die the chair becomes hers. Nayop keeps it by the door in case. *Shou Sugi Ban* changes the molecular structure of the wood and it becomes strong through this burning. we take turns with the blow torch, black dragon absorbing light. we sit in its warm embrace, pelvis in serpent's imprint, verdant smell of smoke. we take turns with the glitch, double walkers, a rhythm laced from entropy. we're like us, too.

1977/04/04

By my own vote, I elected to come back to this Earth.

—A. Turiyasangitananda Coltrane, *Monument Eternal*, 44

1917/01/XX

in Hilma af Klint's notebooks i see quartered squares and cubes, sometimes in or along spiraling tubes. the year HaK graduates college, Hertz documents an electromagnetic wave sent between receivers which later develops into radio—a wave beyond standard human vision that travels to space and comes back down to us *Like a Prayer.* she joins the Rosicrucian Cross and the Theosophists. Theosophy considers the fourth dimension a spiritual plane that is part of human life, manifested by our energy, *A mirror of our world to read backwards and upside down.* after the *Paintings for the Temple*, HaK makes a series of paintings focused on the atom within. each atom is represented by a square four times enlarged: *Every Atom has its own midpoint but each midpoint is directly connected to the center of the universe.*

arms red face brown legs blue stepping out of frame. Chiron surfaces in shamanism research as the Wounded Healer. we share a border body, a hole in our foot that never heals, drama. i carry his picture for a year before learning he's actually the other centaur Sagittarius, but i'm that too, two. from the *Kitāb al-Bulhān*, *The Book of Wonders*, in Latin *The Book of Mira.* if you follow it back in time, the drawings develop from Al-Sufi's *The Book of Fixed Stars*, re-illustrated across centuries, the first Chiron mutating until he grows a black ponytail pulled into a bow and four pale pink shanks. he holds a lion. he holds the only planets astronomers believe to be like Earth.

2019/09/12

they give me a question i cannot answer: *WHY IS IT A RECTANGLE?* i toil at the edges but i don't like to determine things. everyone at the gallery is nervous when i pick up the drill. maybe open the center? *Pricks, bruises* into the clear hologram screens, one with the constellation Centaurus, one with a constellation that is Chiron's foot until it falls into another Hemisphere and becomes the Crux, wound as intersection, we reanimate stars' dead light.

2020/09/27

Helen shares a photograph of an ancient Korean shaman funerary board to carry the bodies of the dead. seven holes are cut out of the large rectangle. it is the constellation Chilseong, the stars that bridge the Milky Way and rule the passage between life and death.

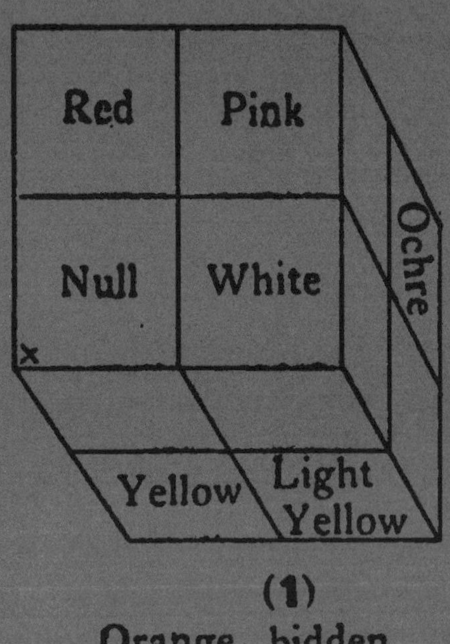

(1)
Orange hidden

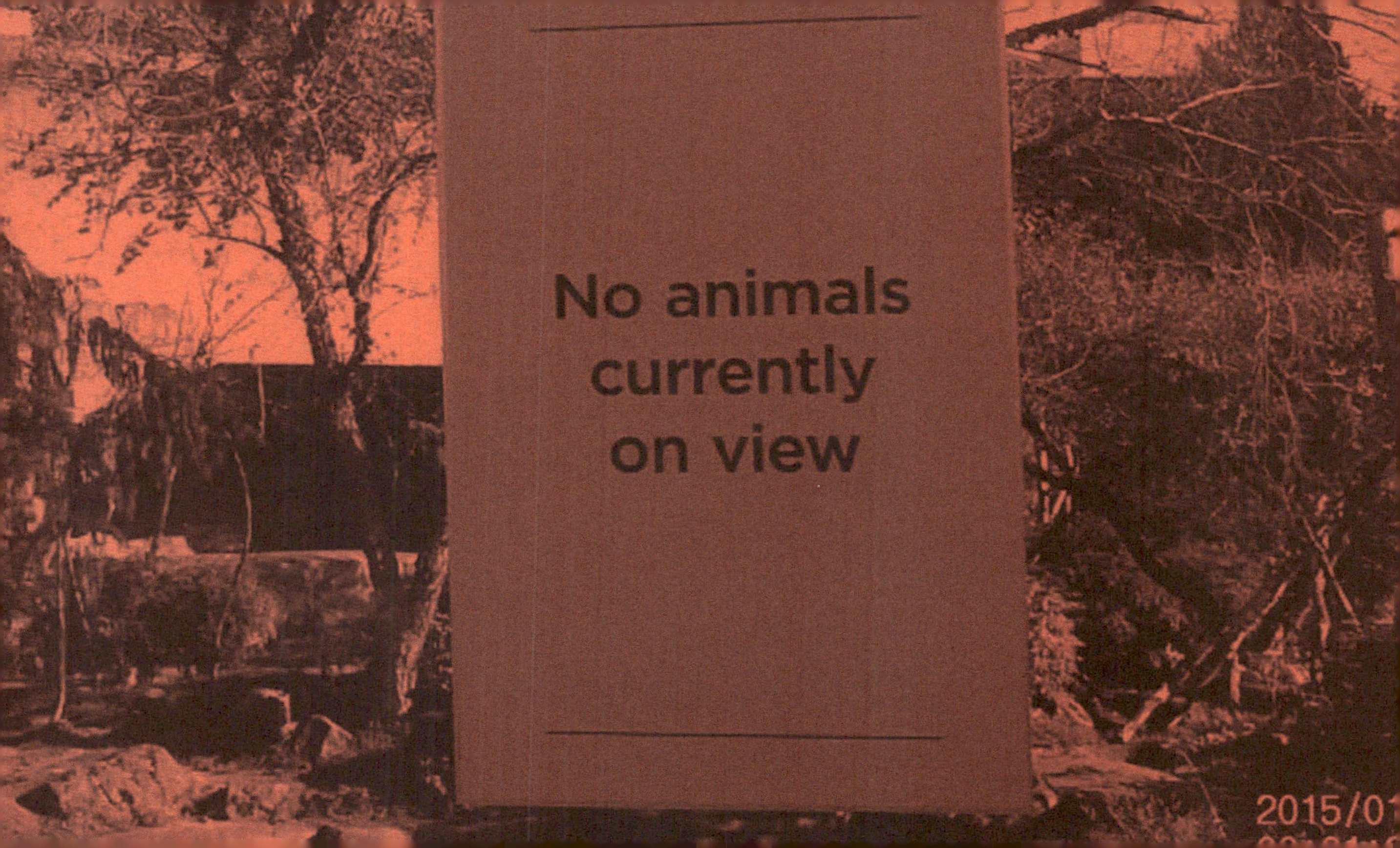
No animals
currently
on view

2021/03/30

[illegible] *SILENCY NEXT STP TERRA INCOGNITA*

TOMORROW OR [illegible] *SERIE NOT SEND AND CHERISH IS*

STARS MOVE

2021/03/22

Joan runs a karaoke night during the day. we meet on an island and she calls me *hyung*, but she is everyone's brother and she lives in Nayop's city where we run into each other each time and i lose my driver's license each time and Joan chooses my songs each time.
now she is in the ICU. Joan asks us for a song to dream. i turn on the tube and for the first time since December, the sonic transmission returns. this time the voices speak at length in Korean: it is 1540 AM Radio Korea. moving the tube, singing into it, creates resonance.
i bring it to the desert with Saewon and Kwonyin and here it makes only the sound of an EKG. empty orchestra. *Bells peal to sky.*

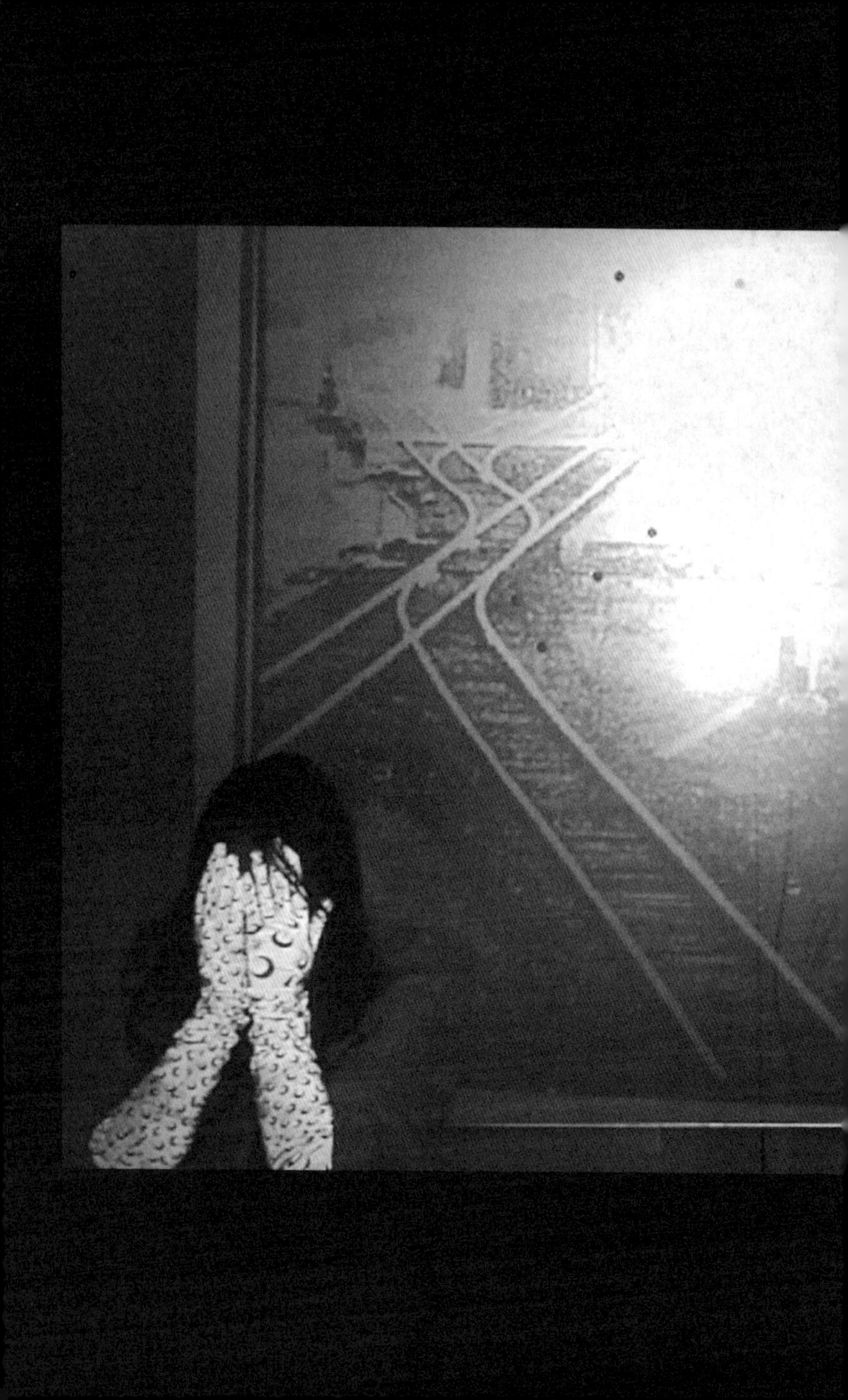

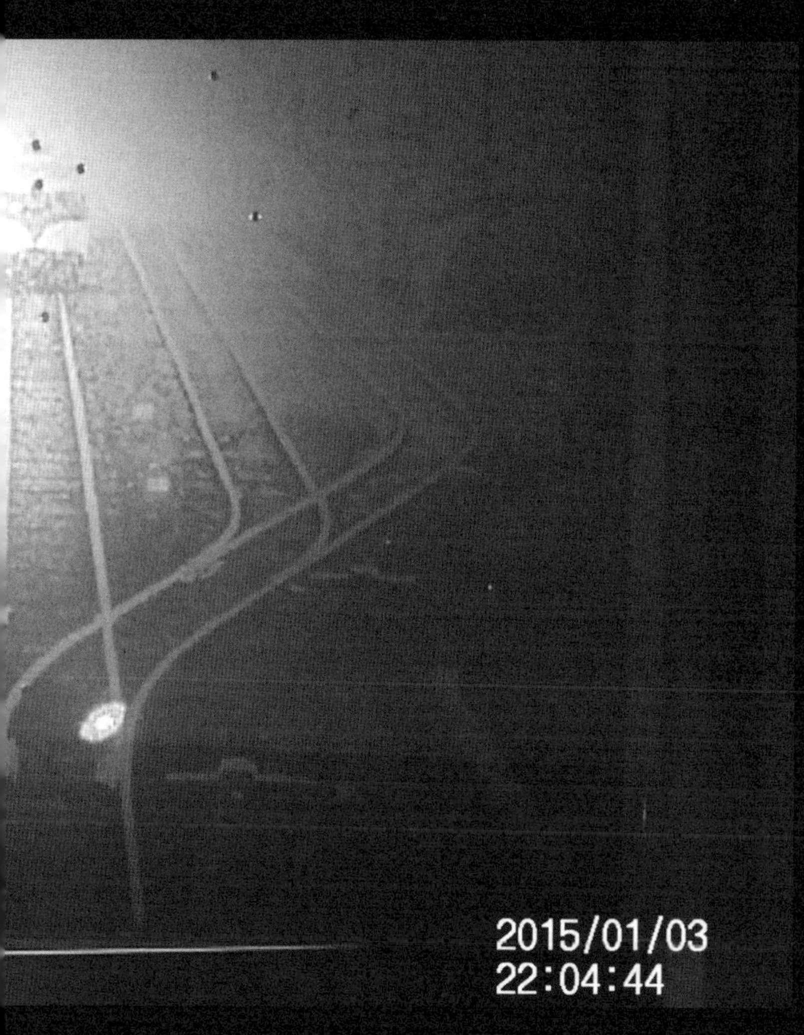
2015/01/03
22:04:44

2021/09/02

sometimes when i move closer to the tube or touch something nearby it gets louder, quieter. when i throw it on the ground the impact can echo, repeat into a melody, but sometimes it doesn't notice me at all. on only a handful of attempts, only holding vowels, i sing into the microphone during the broadcast and it hears my voice. the radio swells as if the host has taken a deep breath mid-sentence, the frequency, we, jump, fold, *SERPENT TENSE*. an opened jawed floral pattern wound round body's bag and lose the beginning. a contrapunctual curtain rising.

2021/03/30

I'll Be Missing You (feat.112)

2021/04/04

Saewon starts a collective meditation laboratory for the flowers in the desert. doing this work in groups is ecstatic, like a song each of us remembers different parts to. there is no door because we are bigger than the room. with this flower we don't speak for a long time. it becomes clear that everyone is crying. Joshua Tree's ancient flower tells me, *VIOLENCE IS THE CRUDEST TECHNOLOGY FOR TRAVELING FROM THE BODY. IT WAS DONE TO US WITH THE IDEA THAT WE WOULD NOT FIND OUR WAY BACK. WE MUST LEARN THE OTHER METHODS TO RETURN BY WILL. THE MOVEMENT OF EVERYTHING SPIRALS BACK AND FORTH. PASSAGE IS OUR BIRTH RITE.*

2020/02/11
Brooke goes to Minneapolis with her Luo Pan and does a reading of the gallery for the next exhibition.

HEXAGRAM 44: Gou / Coming to Meet
Above Heaven ☰
Below Wind ☴
The Hexagram indicates a situation in which the principle of darkness, after having been eliminated, furtively and unexpectedly obtrudes again from within and below. Of its own accord the female principle comes to meet the male. It is an unfavorable and dangerous situation. The maiden is powerful. One should not marry such a maiden. The rise of the inferior element is pictured in the image of a bold girl who lightly surrenders herself and thus seizes power. This would not be possible if the light element had not come halfway. The inferior thing seems so harmless and inviting that a man delights in it; it looks so small and weak that he imagines he may dally with it and come to no harm.

i ask if she thinks this has to do with the Coronavirus. *What?*

2021/04/16

(where is ecstasy?) *SUPINE GERMINAL TERRASTATIS WIND*

NULL NUMB TUBULAR TURBINE ACCEL XL (what is supine?)

SEED CHOREOGRAPHIC THICK

TREMBLE IMAGE TONGUED

2001/03/XX

elle est comme le vent
elle chevauche la nuit à côté de moi
elle me conduit à travers le clair de lune
seulement pour me brûler avec le soleil

There has come to my being the most auspicious time to fulfill a divine command, one which I had let go without a concrete manifestation for many years. This command is an assignment and an honor for me to write: a book based upon the soul's realizations in Absolute Consciousness and its spiritual relationships with the Supreme One. I am deeply and truly thankful, and I will be eternally grateful to the great Sovereign Supreme Lord, always and forevermore.

Turiyasangitananda
(Alice Coltrane)

April 4, 1977
Los Angeles, California

2021/04/04

with Eliza the guides tell me to *PULL OUT THE EROTIC IN CHA'S WORK* and if i can't do this *NONE OF IT WILL BE WORTH IT.*

2021/02/27

when i ask Nayop if i can start using her name officially she laughs. she says her father gave her Mira to use in America, but she never did and that's why she gave it to me. she tells me her favorite name comes from a girl who quit the factory and leaves her notebook behind. these are the initials she uses when ordering coffee. Nayop says the name makes sense because of a dream she just has about me: *You find an invisible door in the wall. You go to a square space, and it looks like nothing but it is something. You pull out a square sheet 4 ft. wide. You're smiling. You open it and there is a smaller sheet 2 ft. wide. Big sheet and small sheet represent the circle of life: family, change, relation, from baby to adult, pure spirit. They're both you.* she says i should show people the squares. *Simple objects make people think more. Rather than art you turn into philosopher. Some degree you are using the same energy. This time is very meaningful for people. They are searching for friends, lovers, family. They are lost but they can fill the small square themself.* she says the dream is a sign i am making progress and so is the name.

2021/07/23

Cha's film archives open for the first time since quarantine. i watch the raw footage she began for *White Dust*; the scenes are different from her notes. instead of the airplane shots there is a scene at an amusement park with a small plane ride. escape, empire, migration, and entertainment collapse. many shots are entrances, pathways. it's the first time i hear her voice, looping back across itself again and again, lapsing through languages, staggering across the stage in assembly, chorus. i read her book on film, *Apparatus*. she uses the word *contrapuntal* to describe the sovereignty of sound and vision, the rejection of immersion, the hyperpresence in dislocation. amidst all the footage, there is a single outtake of her laughing.

1977/XX/XX

Nayop arrives to the United States after being married some years.
the immigration office splits her name in two:
she becomes first name Na middle name Yop
she does not become a citizen
the green card the social security the telemarketers all ask for Na.
all the years i answer
yes, this is Na.
my husband is dead, can you take his name away?

1982/12/20

a negative heirloom. 巫 *SSSS TWIN BENEATH SKIN*, wall, world. *Mu* from nothing from dance from death is how shamanism is called. waves across the line *TEMPO OF GODS NOT GODS NOT GODS IS THIS A HOUSE ARE THESE 4 WALLS FREEDOM DUMB DUMB DUMB*. when we return next to Whore Hill next to Homo Hill next to the Base there is a road that becomes dirt at the door, the long way to school. rite Kut, ride knife, death does not die *FECUND*. no one, she is 10,000. when i say *Mu* the look is repulsion. when i say he is American she is Korean the look is repulsion. both looks policies, poiesis, *Punctum can be ill-bred*. errant wound, under the skin a fruit.

2020/12/09

from the Latin *translat-* or "carried across." when i am a child Nayop refuses to speak to doctors in English anymore. i repeat her English to them which they choose to understand. they say "phrene" as in mind, "schizo" as in split. eventually she refuses altogether. when Nayop tells me the voices flash on a window i don't know i will make one yet, but weeks later for the exhibition in Seoul it's the only part of the museum the other artists don't want, don't see, the glass hallway between rooms. *Mudang, in relation to Chinese, referring to the hall,* 堂 *tang, of a shaman.* to project onto it while still seeing through i must apply a film. the ones i find are all called *hologram, from Greek holos- or* "whole." when you cut a photograph it splits. when you cut a hologram it multiplies. the (w)hole is in every part. when Na is sixty-five and i apply for Medicare i become conscious of her voice. one day Nayop starts to sing *Come to My Window.* she says, *Melissa is not like other women. Her voice is husky, like traditional Pansori singer.*

And i would stand inside my hell
And i would hold the hand of death
Just to reach you

i try husky for Na.

2020/12/27

(what if I record Cla's final scene?) *TESSERACT PULSE SPOOLS NUDGE* (what spools?) *TIME MENDABLE NASCENT*

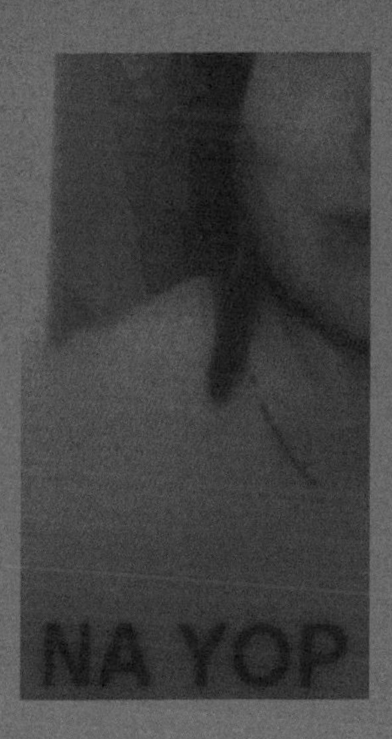
NA YOP

2017/11/01

Inevitably, the performer of the Abandoned is expected to have the experience of "hearing" the spirits of the dead who are called ghosts, spirits, or gods, in addition to having the experience of going through a penance within a life of ordeal, suffering from shaman-sickness, or undergoing with her own body a world of illusions... At that moment, somewhere within her, she can feel a sense of opening of a women's world that has the hearing of death. She is hearing the femininity...

2021/07/21

The Answer Is Blowing in the Wind

Knocking on Heaven's Door

Video Killed the Radio Star

We Are the World

2021/07/09

(how to listen?) *STIR OR UTTER SIGNAL TRANCE*

2021/10/20

The Sound of Silence

Come Undone

Like a Rock

Like a Prayer

2020/01/15

trying to learn if radiation will help our cat i find that in the 1980s semioticians are tasked with creating a sign for America's buried nuclear waste that can be understood ten thousand years in the future. they propose that myth is the only language that survives. and cats genetically modified to change colors around radiation will be signified by culture. the plan is sadistically awkward, human, falls apart. the spent fuel is still waiting at the power plants. cats LOL. the largest pile is at the San Onofre Nuclear Generator Station. SONGS is in the city where i just start teaching. SONGS sits on a beach and is in the movies, in *Cloud Atlas*, about lives that intersect for generations. we watch it for our friend who's cat passes away, shining gray light. the night before she knows she's pregnant.

2019/01/22

Brooke suggests a constellation and i don't know the verb but i am gathering points of light. i take Yuneun's circular Baguazhang martial arts class a year ago, based on the same trigrams as Feng Shui. it's walking in a circle, almost impossible. now i see Yunuen leads constellations. when i learn the chair has a matching table there's a flash of us moving round its round form. Nayop says i can have the table but calls back and says, *You can't take it because of the Atomic Bomb.* her father's photograph is on the table and now he's part of it. what does this have to do with the bomb? *He was studying in Japan and had to evacuate back to Korea and become a farmer.* forty-four years before we move to Hiroshima. is that why i only remember him being angry? *Yes!* what if i heal the table?

2006/XX/XX

What we need to recall is how the "thisness" of this table does not, as it were, belong to it: what is particular about this table, what we can tell through its biography, is also what allows us to tell a larger story: a story not only of "things" changing hands, but of how things come to matter by taking shape through and in the labor of others.

—Sara Ahmed, *Queer Phenomenology: Orientations, Objects, Others*, 44

2020/02/08

the guide at SONGS announces this is the final tour because the plant is being dismantled the next day and all the fuel rods will be buried here. am i the last person to see this?

2020/03/06

the LA River comes up every day for weeks so this is where i ask Yunuen to meet me and the table. the river is paved in concrete for almost a century, ecology adapting from flood plane towards freeway, but water still finds its course. like SONGS, the LA River plays itself on TV. mythic, thick. Yunuen walks across it.

2020/03/25

seven thousand gallons of sewage leak from SONGS into the Pacific.

2020/06/26

Saewon and i go to the ocean to make a flower essence. waves come in and a little Dixie cup spits out at our feet. crows descend and take our food. does the Earth want a potion and chips? i guess it's rude we never offered. the ancestors tell me to heal the water but i don't know how. then they show me Yunuen at the river, glitch pouring open into monstrosity nine heads nine hands as we spills out of ourself, to the sea. did we do it in reverse?

2022/02/14

i find a recording from three years ago when i ask Nayop to recite poetry. between the lines she starts talking about a song she hears, a woman singing *She don't want to love right now.* when do you think she's gonna love? Nayop repeats the line from *Dictee, Until in all cavities she is flesh until in all cavities she is flesh until in all cavities she is flesh* and asks, *Flesh means gone? Like disappear?*

2019/XX/XX

What it means to be at home in your own skin turns out to signal the necessary distance between ontology and its ornaments.

—Anne Anlin Cheng, *Ornamentalism*, 44

2022/04/21

I Left My Heart in San Francisco

Brown Eyed Girl

1875/08/24

there are twenty-two Asian women standing at the edge of legal personhood in the US. banned from entering the port of San Francisco for appearing *lewd* because they are unaccompanied, unclaimed by men, the men who are brought to the US to build the transcontinental railroad tracks for which time itself will become standardized.

2021/12/26

Character #2 is at the moment of the return, to retrieve events past (marked within the chronology of Time, which functions as punctuation, as marked points in Time). The return re-marks the locations, points in memory, re-peat the Past sequences.

—Theresa Hak Kyung Cha, on *White Dust from Mongolia*

2021/04/05

(where is the erotic?) *SENSORY CRYSTALLINE AAAAAAAH ON AND ON LACED VEINS STACCATO* (what to sense?) *SHADOW LANGUAGE ERUPT TOUCH TITRATE*

1896/01/25

before a girl and a gun is a train. the first train arrives on the screen, the image moving into the theater, bodies moving away from the image. in her notes for *White Dust from Mongolia,* Cha does not describe a train arriving, it is the tracks that return. Character #2 moves from the theater into the screen onto the tracks to meet Character #1 beyond the fourth wall where we can't see, rewinding cinema's original spell

taeguk

she rides the dark between frames

2020/12/06

i choose two chrome motorcycle rearview mirrors after learning shamans use round mirrors in ritual. i get these for Changok's border crossing, for their ability to see into the past. they hang in the back of the final scene of *White Dust* i perform, witnesses on the wall. i keep trying for months but still don't really know how to use them and eventually leave the mirrors on the floor. here they catch the sun from the exhaust pipe in the ceiling and shine. are they for reflecting light? *The principle of darkness, after having been eliminated, furtively and unexpectedly obtrudes again from within and below.*

2021/08/28

Grace shows me the two identical statues of Puck, smug demon fairies in tailcoat and top hat each holding up a hand mirror. they guard the building where Cha is murdered, now owned and occupied by the Kushner family. a final scene. *We must evacuate the building.*

2017/XX/XX

Love is a "two-scene," a theater meant for a duo, to paraphrase Badiou. Interrupting the isolated perspective of the One, it makes the world arise anew from the vantage point of the Other, or of Difference... It generates a "rupture," a "hole," in the order of the Habitual and of the Same... Eros manifests itself as the revolutionary yearning for an entirely different way of loving and another kind of society. Thereby, it remains faithful to what is yet to come.

—Byung-Chul Han, *The Agony of Eros*, 44-45

2021/09/13

for weeks i meet Cha in a theater. we take turns showing scenes of a movie. sometimes she projects red and sometimes i do. sometimes i appear, played by someone else. sometimes a shape or texture   the other's negative in relief   a cell cupped by the image around it. then we double project. a Möbius filmstrip holding hands. today we each show one side of a crescent moon. knifed night smiles wax to wane, becomes hole in the center, *a hole in time, the object of retrieval.* the hole is three-dimensional and slides out of the screen.

2021/09/20

on the September full mirror *Chuseok* for the ancestors i travel to New York. by day i track the streets in front of Puck to find where his reflection catches. i mention the ritual at dinner before i go and my friends say it's scary to go alone, to wait, and i admit there is no one to hold the camera. it's hard to plan for what i'm doing, i don't know what it is. Nayop says, *You can't plan a miracle.* i return to the theater, i tell Cha SORRY on the marquee and she writes back *OKAY.* for all the weeks after i worry it is a mistake, that i let her down.

2021/09/06

Mr. Sandman

Mr. Postman

Mr. Lonely

Mr. Blue

2021/10/20

this moon i begin planning for the next. if i return to the Puck Building in November it will be a half blood lunar eclipse. only infrared sun will reach the moon at 4 am, the longest eclipse since 1440. i ask for a sign and let *Dictee* open:

Inside the eclipse. Both. Fulmination and concealment of light.
Imminent crossing, face to face moon before the sun pronounces.
All. This. Time.
Carrier, you hold in your palm the silver white spirit the lustre mass quiver
Red as never been the color that already was before it's exhibition into sight

2021/11/17

it was an orange day the stripes sliced in sky. i tell Bobby don't you know i love you? and they say, *I don't want to know what I already know about love.* which is why a cat is also the shadow they exit through. the sun stands still and we are punctuated. Hiroko says, *Our nails are the wildest part of us left* so i dye nail for 내일. when we are little the saying is, *If your nails are still red by the first snowfall you will be with your true love.* anciently the 봉선화 flower stain is a protection spell. i meet her claws vermillion crescent tipped days becoming tiger since solstice and tonight it's all i can do i still do not know tomorrow *nael.* then an email comes for the *Dictee* reading marathon. it's been moved to the next eclipse, the fourth. they choose a passage for me: *Red as never been.*

2016/05/07

instead of the funeral i get an infrared camera to feel the night-blooming cactus flower behind my house and dance Hiroko's Butoh score which i only record with a microphone. the days were a constant vigil, vigilance. i start to sense the particles in everything handfuls of dust making jokes   this one is about us, poured right through the punchline. total touch   test tomb. it is not something you can look at.

2012/12/06

Could I manage to surrender to the expectant silence of a question with no answer? from off screen Nayop's voice is doubled, *Yeah! Yeah!*

2021/03/24

(to live in death?) *TERRA PATINA YOU WERE THERE AIR AIR AIR STUTTER AGAIN AND AGAIN SEER SEAR EAR SONOROUSSSSSSSS SU SINEW YOU*

2021/11/19
Mudang use the ancient *Sam Taeguk*
beyond the black and white inertia of change
threshold's pulse a third element
a body between Heaven and Earth
If you take your camera to the border you can cross
there are six sets of solid lines crossing the
streets around the building
Heaven's trigram at Hell's mouth
meets me *Inferior element, Weak, Lewd*
halfway at 4 am.
Oh, what fools these mortals be!
blood mirrored below prayer's frequency
subrosa
SHRED air opens knock-off
wind coat made in Korea
infinity's seam showing
i am bigger than i am
tree, sentry, promise carries the glitch
sun done and dimming behind Earth all broken lines
Moon coiled and hinged
becoming red on white, becoming heat not light
the negative heirloom the hyper feminine superposition
CHILSEUNG SUNG SINGING TINTINABULAR CULL SOUL
TELL YOU: RIDE ON INTO SELF TIL THE SAME CHANNEL
SOURCE CENTRIFUGAL FORCE CONTAMINATION
잘자 CODA 생일 축하합니다

NEITHER

NOR

HOW DO I ENTE

utter
chalya
THE TESSERACT

Thanks to B, Lutz Bacher, Ohan Breiding, Theresa Hak Kyung Cha, Grace M. Cho, Chloe Chung, Abigail Collins, Aja Daashuur, Hayden Dunham, Laura Ellis, Simone Forti, Bramashakti Fudail, Mariah Garnett, Sara Gernsbacher, Sho Halajian, EJ Hill, Hanna Hur, Helen Hye-Sook Hwang, Brooke Intrachat, Ryan Kelly, Grace Kredell, Kwonyin, Azalea Lee, Young Joo Lee, Mikail, Monty, Nayop, Saewon Oh, K-Sue Park, Litia Perta, Pil, Ariana Reines, Yunuen Rhi, Brooke Smith, Eliza Swann, Hiroko Tamano, Lanka Tattersall, Turiyasangitananda, Tutankhamun, Genevieve Yim, Chi Young, Laurie Weeks, Marty Windahl, and the 10,000 spirits.

Thanks to Talia Linz and Artspace Sydney; the Theresa Hak Kyung Cha Conceptual Art Archive, Berkeley Art Museum, University of California; Sophie Mörner, Taylor Trabulus, and Company Gallery; Geneva Skeen, Simon Leung, Satyan Devadoss, and Fulcrum Arts; Ellie Lee and GYOPO; Kathy Cho and The Kitchen; John Rasmussen, Megan McCready, Kelsey Olson, and Midway Contemporary Art; Christine Y. Kim and LACMA; Suzy Halajian and Oregon Contemporary and Actual Size Gallery; Paul Soto and Parkview/Paul Soto; Kristan Kennedy and PICA; Pascal Storz and Provence; Hyewon Lee and Space XX; Leire Urbeltz, Elina Juopperi, Namjoo Huh, and the Seoul Museum of Art Nanji; Rachel Valinsky, Kyla Arsadjaja, Flo Li, Juwon Jun, and Wendy's Subway; Adrienne Edwards, David Breslin, Melanie Taylor, Megan Heuer, Soyoung Yoon, and the Whitney Museum of American Art.

The Book of Na

Document Series #10
First Edition, 2022
Edition of 750 copies
ISBN: 978-8-9863375-0-0
Library of Congress Control Number: 2022943861

Edited by Rachel Valinsky
Editorial assistance by Juwon Jun and Flo Li
Designed by Kyla Arsadjaja
Typeset in Times New Roman and Arial
Printed at Grafiche Veneziane, Italy

Distributed in Europe and the UK
by Antenne Books
www.antennebooks.com

Published by Wendy's Subway
379 Bushwick Avenue
Brooklyn, NY 11206
www.wendyssubway.com

Wendy's Subway is a non-profit reading room, writing space, and independent publisher located in Brooklyn.

The Document Series is an interdisciplinary publishing initiative that highlights works by time-based artists in printed form.

This publication is supported, in part, by public funds from the New York City Department of Cultural Affairs in partnership with the City Council of New York, the Andy Warhol Foundation for the Visual Arts, and the Robert Rauschenberg Foundation.

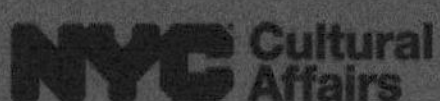

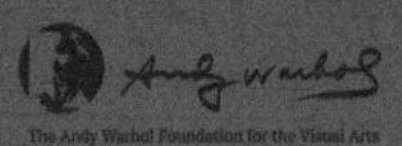

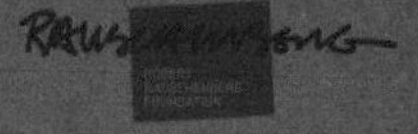